TOTAL RUNNING

ALL ABOUT THE MENTAL
AND SPIRITUAL SIDE
OF RUNNING

TOTAL RUNNING

ALL ABOUT THE MENTAL AND SPIRITUAL SIDE OF RUNNING

by **Jim Lilliefors**

WILLIAM MORROW AND COMPANY, INC.
NEW YORK   1979

BOOK DESIGN   CARL WEISS

Library of Congress Catalog Card Number 79-4429

ISBN 0-688-03457-8

Printed in the United States of America.

2   3   4   5   6   7   8   9   10

DEDICATED

TO PEOPLE

WHO RUN

ACKNOWLEDGMENTS

Special thanks to Bob Bender, who edited *Total Running* and helped to guide it from an idea into its present form.

And to James Marlin, whose aim is still true.

CONTENTS

ACKNOWLEDGMENTS   7

ONE   : TOTAL RUNNING   15
TWO   : RUNNING AND RELAXATION   33
THREE : RUNNING AND CONTENTMENT   55
FOUR   : RUNNING AND SUCCESS   71
FIVE   : RUNNING AND STRESS   89
SIX   : RUNNING AND MEDITATION   101
SEVEN : RUNNING AND ZEN   117
EIGHT : RUNNING AND SPIRITUALISM   133
NINE   : RUNNING AND THE ASTRAL
          SENSATION   149
TEN   : RUNNING AND THE FOUNTAIN
          OF YOUTH   165

BIBLIOGRAPHY   187

"The last temptation is the greatest treason
To do the right deed for the wrong reason."

—T. S. Eliot

TOTAL
RUNNING

ALL ABOUT THE MENTAL
AND SPIRITUAL SIDE
OF RUNNING

TOTAL RUNNING

OF THE MORE THAN TWENTY MILLION AMERICANS WHO are running today, most who start do so for the wrong reasons, with the wrong attitude, and tend to lose interest after a few weeks or months. Many quit. This is usually because they become concerned with superficial goals such as time and distance and never discover the more profound mental benefits that running offers.

Total Running is about those mental benefits and how you can achieve them by changing your approach to running. Total Running is not running to lose weight or to protect yourself against heart attack (although these are certainly by-products of Total Running), but instead it is running to become more relaxed, content, successful, and even more spiritually aware. A 1978 survey I took on the mental aspects of running revealed that all of these benefits are available if you approach running properly. Among the results of the survey of three hundred runners, all readers of *Runner's World* magazine, were these: 79 percent of the runners ran, in part at least, to relieve tension; 56 percent were less depressed since they started running; 57 percent felt better afterward if they ran when depressed. Many of those surveyed gave detailed explanations of how running had altered their habits and positively affected their lifestyles; these accounts are included throughout the book.

Interestingly, I arrived at the concept of Total Running by mistake. First I tried the more common approaches to running and encountered the usual problems. I quit running several times over the past eight years before the concept of Total Running crystallized in my mind. And, as I've found, Total Running is really an approach to all of life, a revolution of attitude.

I began my running in high school as a competitive distance runner with grandiose aspirations. After a moderately successful first year at it, I transformed into a hopeless zealot, running 100 miles a week year round. Superficially, at least, it paid off; even though I wasn't thoroughly enjoying the stringency of my running, I was improving my times and winning some races.

But as with many beginning runners, the satisfaction of my running was based more on the accomplishment of goals than on the running itself. I was more concerned with achieving than I was with experiencing. I made certain I never did fewer than two workouts a day during the week —one aerobic run and one interval workout—and I sometimes piled up as many as four or five workouts in a day. The pinnacle of my rigors came in July of 1973 when I ran 620 miles—an average of 20 per day. Although I didn't enjoy that month a whole lot, I achieved my goal.

As my training became more difficult, I began to learn about the drawbacks of strict goal-oriented thinking. My satisfaction with running wasn't increasing correspondingly with my mileage; rather, running became less enjoyable. My energy, mental as well as physical, was directed toward one less-than-fulfilling end—the attainment of a fixed number of miles. I got my satisfaction more from the statistics than from the time spent attaining the statistics.

I kept a journal of my running and reviewed it frequently. The figures—mile-per-day average, interval times —interested me far more than the feelings—intense euphorias, severe lethargy. Had I paid more attention to mood than to statistics, I might have known I was heading for trouble.

It was a time of obsession. A typical day began at 5:30 A.M. when I went out into the silent darkness for a five-mile run. Before noon, I'd have done another three miles, including a dozen wind sprints. The serious running came later, in the afternoons, when I'd do either a fast timed distance run of seven to fifteen miles or a series of track intervals. On weekends I did long runs, once going forty-four miles in one afternoon.

But as many runners do, I was enduring the running rather than experiencing it, experimenting with it, and enjoying it. I followed schedules rather than doing what felt best. I forced myself through runs that didn't feel right and ended runs that felt wonderful just because I'd met the quota of my training schedule.

Fantasy and reality met somewhere in 1974, after almost four years of constant, intense training. I was on a treadmill of good and bad feelings about what I was doing, always related to goals. My motivation remained constant, but my confidence wavered constantly. This was because my satisfaction was dependent not on day-to-day experiences but on the achievement of long-term goals. For four years, my life revolved around running, specifically around my running goals.

Ironically, just three-fourths of a year after averaging twenty miles a day, I quit running entirely. I had just run my fastest mile race, but it didn't mean much. The euphorias had disappeared. For eight months I didn't run a step, and didn't particularly miss it.

Although my example is somewhat extreme, I was similar to many runners in that I was running primarily to achieve goals and noticeable results. I sacrificed many of the good feelings running could bring to the rest of my life.

I went back to running in a very subdued manner, mostly just because I felt guilty for being out of shape. I ran just two to three miles at a time, three or four times a week. There was an initial iridescent joy at rediscovering running, but the sensation soon became, again, less than gratifying. I continued, though, to keep in shape, unenthusiastically, sporadically, more out of guilt than out of desire.

Although I didn't realize it at the time, I had just been through the process of accepting and rejecting running for the two most common reasons: the fleeting satisfaction of goal achievement and guilt for being out of shape.

But I came back to running for another reason, when I realized that I could enjoy it without recording my mileage, when I began to experience the mental effects that were possible. That became Total Running.

I returned to running when I discovered it could help my state of mind and my work, when I realized it could be a relaxing means of self-exploration. The procedure of this discovery was simple: I began running with a more relaxed attitude and Total Running found me.

Now, I no longer make myself finish a ten-mile run if it doesn't feel right, but I frequently set out for a planned half-hour run and turn it into a ten-miler because it feels good.

Total Running is a free-form, goalless approach to running that can positively affect your attitudes, motivation, and life-style. More than that, as presented here, it encompasses a progression to deep states of relaxation, meditation, Zen attitude, and a greater significance to your life. Whereas a traditional approach to running might make you fitter, this approach can change your life-style. It can give you greater self-confidence and a new willingness to experiment. It can show you the perils of self-doubt and make you more aware of your potential. It can add a sense of order to your life-style and a feeling of meaning to your life. And it can make you a more productive worker and less of a procrastinator.

In the first half of the book, the basis of Total Running is developed through relaxation exercises. Chapters discuss the impact of Total Running on contentment, success, and stress. In the second half is a progression through meditation and Zen to the more profound states of mind possible through Total Running.

RHYTHM

If you are able to run two or three miles, you are ready to experiment with Total Running. Start by trying a few runs alone through an unfamiliar locale. Don't think about how far you're going or how fast. Concentrate not on finishing but just on experiencing your surroundings. Don't put any pressure on yourself. If the run feels uncomfortable, stop. Walk if you feel like it. And if you want to go farther than usual, by all means do that.

Chances are this approach will have effects very different from what you are accustomed to. This will help acquaint you with the rhythm of Total Running, the attitude necessary for the positive effects it can begin to have on your life-style. And it may clear away some of the cynicism or dislike that you had toward running.

The most important prerequisite to developing Total Running is acquiring a proper attitude. To accept a new approach to running is to reject completely the stereotype of running as drudgery.

Eventually, Total Running can become natural, second nature, even though initially it might seem uncomfortable and unpredictable. It is a progression which you begin when you go out and practice running with no goals.

Janet Pearson, a marathoner from Washington (and wife of American 50-mile record holder Jim Pearson), described how running became positively integrated into her life-style: "At first, it was a chore to get out and run every day—especially in bad weather—and sometimes I would skip a day or two here and there. Now, after four years, I don't think about running, I just do it. When it's icy and blowing, I never think of not doing it. It's just a part of me."

When you run without goals, your doubts and discomforts disappear because you are only running when and how you want to. Running ceases being an obligation. Eventually you'll reach the point where running is as basic as eating and sleeping and the urge to run will generally direct you toward your most enjoyable runs by naturally leading you away from the stresses of your life. Just enjoying running is the first step in Total Running.

As running becomes natural, runners often find that what they previously have taken for granted becomes special. A run down a crowded evening street can develop new dimensions if you have just spent four hours reading in a dusty room; store lights will suddenly glow and wiggle, shop signs may beg for personal relevance, traffic lights will spread strangely animated patches of yellow, red, and green across black pavement.

"Sometimes I'll be running along the same road I do four days a week," said Los Angeles runner Mario J., "and suddenly it'll seem different. I'll notice things, like the surface of the road or the clouds in the sky. I just open up."

There will be such exceptional runs, though the more regular effect will be a relaxed, calm peace of mind that might carry over into your non-running life.

Some find that running the same time each day is valuable; free-form running can still be developed on a regular schedule.

A runner from Gary, Indiana, offered this example: "I find that when I can adopt a simple, but highly consistent running program, I have the most fun at it. I don't always have to worry about fitting in my run because I just do it at a regular time. I believe that a regular schedule is best also because it allows a break in your work schedule. If you fit it in like I do, during lunch hour, it relieves the pressure of the morning's work. I think it's best to fit running in where it will do some good besides just being fun."

Whether it is best to run at one specific time varies with

the runner; each must find his or her own rhythm through experimentation.

EVOLUTION

The Total Running approach isn't something I invented; it's just something I stumbled upon. Actually, it probably goes back to the earliest days of humankind. Cave paintings of running indicate that even cavemen probably derived a sense of gentle satisfaction from running.

Since early in this century, sandlot running clubs have existed, devoted to running more as a relaxing, enjoyable activity than as physical fitness or a form of competition. In the 1960's, Dr. Kenneth Cooper, in his book *Aerobics*, cited a number of instances in which physical exercise was a major factor in easing psychological disorders.

Perhaps the most obvious manifestation of a relaxed approach to running came from Frank Shorter, winner of the 1972 Olympic marathon (the first American to win the race since 1908). It was Shorter's victory that did much to create the current interest in long-distance running. Besides a fluid style that caught the American imagination, Shorter's approach to competitive running was considerably different from that of past United States distance runners. When asked why he ran so much, instead of talking about the "pain equals gain" ethic that many competitive runners still subscribe to, he said, "I imagine that I wouldn't do it if I didn't enjoy it."

EUPHORIA

When you approach running as an experiment, one of the first effects you encounter will be occasional euphorias.

Later, through the progression of Total Running, this effect should expand into a more uniform sensation.

Dr. Thaddeus Kostrubala, author of *The Joy of Running*, and other medical authorities say that the euphoria of running happens after thirty minutes as this is the point when serum levels in the brain and the hormone norepinephrine have increased sufficiently to make the so-called runner's high possible. However, many runners have euphoric sensations much sooner than the thirty-minute point.

Scientific explanations have yet to expound on the reasons for the sometimes profound, generally elusive nature of the running euphoria. It is here, in our fascination with the mystery of the widely varying effects of running, that interest has been focused.

Though some runners describe the feelings running produces as uniform, most experience peaks and canyons. Fifty-three percent of those surveyed said they have a few exceptional runs when they experience "visions," "insights," or "revelations." Fifty-nine percent weren't able to tell beforehand when these extreme sensations were likely to occur.

These moments may allow a person a glimpse of the possibilities his life-style has hidden. Those who believe in a spiritual dimension to running say these peaks are their connection with God and their clue to the rightness of the world.

Thaddeus Kostrubala described these sensations in *The Joy of Running*:

> You may be lucky to get one of those especially vivid moments that becomes your private personal treasure for the rest of your life. The senses seem to increase in alertness. All

of them respond: sight, hearing, touch, taste, smell, and position. The experience is something like a dream. We may not understand it and may only be able to guess at some of the symbolism that is brought to our consciousness.

Many of those who responded to the survey mentioned such special runs and subsequent attempts to recapture those sensations, mostly unsuccessfully. Part of the magic of running euphorias is their elusiveness.

FREQUENCY

The running euphoria will sometimes be surprisingly intense, other times it will seem strangely absent. The most essential factor in whether a euphoria occurs seems to be the ability of the runner to relax, mentally as well as physically, to let the mind drift freely, to be free of anxiety.

Several runners in the survey said they experience the running euphoria almost every time they go out; these people are probably the most relaxed. Others find it only occasionally, though their euphoria is probably more profound than that of those who get "high" on a regular basis. All seem in agreement that the most profound experiences are seldom if ever predictable.

According to Peter W., an Iowa psychiatrist, "Running provides me with a regular altered state of consciousness. . . . But I have learned that I can't seek the altered state while running. . . . It was after trying to observe more closely what was happening to me that I suddenly had many fewer experiences of it. The more I tried to capture the unconscious consciously, the more elusive it became."

Dr. William Glasser has written: "We are all descended from those who ran to stay alive, and this need to run has been genetically programmed into our brains. When we gain the endurance to run long distances easily, then a good run reactivates the ancient neural pattern."

This neural pattern, which shows the great human potential each of us has, perhaps suppressed since childhood, is still available. It is the joy of discovering this neural pattern that changes people's lives once they begin running.

With rediscovery of ancient neural patterns childhood hopes return; neglected dreams often seem possible again. This is why running eases depression—it offers a replacement.

"Running showed me that life is never 'over.' It invigorated me and my thinking," wrote an Allison, Iowa, runner.

Runners frequently report a change in their goals, in life outlook. Many say that if they stop running, the childlike emotions evaporate again. But most don't want to give up this part of their life after they've found it. "I intend to run to my funeral if health permits," is how Norman P., a fifty-year-old runner from Danville, California, describes this reverential dedication to the running sensation.

Runners frequently talk of withdrawal symptoms if they miss a day. Straying from running, even for a few days, sometimes dulls senses, hopes, and ambitions.

THERAPY AND PERSONALITY

As you begin experimenting with the possibilities of running, you may experience a wide variety of emotions. The effects of running may even be so dramatic and unpredictable that extreme personality changes, positive as well as negative, will occur. In a 1978 *Psychology Today* article on running, Dr. William Morgan said that if approached improperly, running could lead to psychological traumas. Dr. Thomas Bassler, a Los Angeles pathologist, has seen several cases in which running a fast marathon has led to irrational behavior and even suicide in the weeks afterward.

Fifty-nine percent of the runners surveyed believed they were "addicted." Dr. John Greist has said of this, "Runners are like the drug addict who goes to . . . get his fix." But there is a clear distinction between addiction to running and drug addiction. Rather than the anxiety and unwanted mental dependency that other addictions produce, running gives reduced worry, a clear mind, and greater achievement.

The replacement of negative addictions has become one of running's major therapeutic values. Rock star Alice Cooper represents a legion of depression-oriented celebrities who recently turned to running. Others include Linda Ronstadt, Brian Wilson, and Ed Asner. Cooper recently went through a rehabilitation program that used running as a substitute for his alcohol addiction.

Dr. Glasser explored the concept of addiction in a study of 700 runners, reporting the results in his book *Positive Addiction*. "The two key questions. 'Do you suffer if you miss a run?' and 'Do you always enjoy your run?' are both answered with an emphatic 'yes,' indicating addiction," Glasser said.

Running, even for competitive athletes, is also a valuable, sometimes crucial escape from many of the pressures and tensions of life. For example, Olympic Trial marathoner Bill Stewart said, "My main goal in training is a contact with myself, a certain flow of energy that is very peaceful and easy. I look forward to these times as a retreat from the manufactured realities of life."

THE RUNNING TOOL

Eventually, there is no reason running shouldn't become a tool, used to correct unproductive attitudes and negative inclinations. This is what Total Running does. Just as there are calculators and computers to solve mathematical problems, running can solve the less scientific, more intuitive types of problems. In fact, in right-handed people, running usually most affects the left side of the brain, its intuitive part.

The opposite is also true: Running may affect the right, more scientific part of the brain, if it is more underdeveloped. This depends, of course, on the individual. Scientific thinkers often say that running allows them to suddenly see the poetry and magic of life; many overly imaginative thinkers say running has made their thinking more rational and lets them solve problems more easily.

In response to the survey, many runners mentioned problem-solving and greater productivity.

George A., of Liverpool, New York, said, "When running in the morning, I often am able to plan my day's activities very clearly and completely. Minor details that otherwise require notes as reminders become precise and easy to remember."

George had been working on an assignment for an educational administration course when he went on a particularly enlightening run: "I had toyed with the assignment for some weeks without any acceptable ideas coming to mind. One night, when running about six miles, I began to think about the project. I did not force my thoughts, but let various ideas filter through my mind. Ideas flowed smoothly, and very quickly a picture of a possible model emerged. The final picture became clearly focused before the end of the run. I was unusually confident of the result. My biggest concern was that I would forget the details before I could finish and write them down."

Runners often finish runs bursting with ideas. Although sometimes not much happens, sometimes there is an eruption of ideas and insights.

TRANSFORMATION

As you continue the experiment of goalless running there will sometimes be days when your run gives an intense positive attitude, when it seems to transcend time and distance. The run provides the proverbial oneness of body and mind, the "blinding light" sensation that sometimes resembles a religious transformation.

Craig W., a Chula Vista, California, runner, described a run he had: "After about an hour, I found myself turning down a dirt road with a field of cows off to my right. The sun was about to set, and the world seemed enveloped in a blue haze. Many rich, organic odors filled my nostrils; the smell of cow dung, the richness of wet ground, and the odor of freshly cut fields. I suddenly found myself with tears streaming down my face and felt an unbelievable powerful force of the rightness of the world and optimism for my life. I glanced down at my legs, which pounded the ground methodically, and I felt the rich summer air fill my lungs. My feelings lasted maybe thirty seconds, after which the tears dried and I returned to the task of moving the physical me over the soil, immeasurably richer for the brief experience that had taken place."

Another runner said, "I'm often a completely different person after running than I was when I started."

The transformation may seem so dramatic, in part, because running conjures up not only the positive depths of a person, but the demons as well. The most profound effects involve coming to an awareness of both these good and evil forces.

In the poll, 49 percent of the runners described running as "spiritual." Some runners specifically mentioned this aspect. One, John M., of New York City, said, "I've come to know myself more completely through running. I learned about the good and the evil, and I feel that running has helped dissipate the evil."

INDIVIDUALISM

The great potential of running stems from the fact that it is perhaps the most free and individualistic of all sports. Team sports demand a specific reaction and sports such as tennis or golf have the distraction of scoring and measurement and the necessity of great concentration. The effects of running are as diverse as the life-style of its participants.

It isn't magical. In fact, it may be the direct opposite of a dictionary definition of magic (though it is often the very real that seems magica¹ to us). The general way

Total Running works is by easing immediate psychological burdens.

While criminal laws and institutions become the refuge of some who aren't able to come to terms with their inner struggle, with their addictions and confusions, running can be a much more effective influence on people, by meditatively calming them. Greater self-understanding is the switch that has turned on so much interest.

Running is winning a massive, frightening battle, the inner human war that Thomas Carlyle described as follows: "Everywhere the human soul stands between a hemisphere of light and another of darkness on the confines of two everlasting hostile empires—Necessity and Free Will." This has become particularly apparent recently, as books and magazines have proclaimed the problems of our inner crises.

Total Running is an experience in self-awareness and heightened perception. It differs from past definitions of running in that they were concerned with running as either physical fitness or as competition. Those who neglect the Total Running aspect of the sport are only using running to benefit their physical health: they ignore the benefits it can have on their psyche. Those who try running and quit are generally the ones who start just to lose a few pounds. To them, running is little different from a fad diet.

Total Running involves an experiment. The total runner approaches the activity without goals, as neither exercise nor ego gratification; these are perhaps by-products along the way, but nothing more.

Olympic marathoner Don Kardong described this type of runner as a poet and a magician who "accepts no limits," making himself "less predictable but infinitely more interesting" than the person with a more scientific approach to running.

Total Running is a subtle, creative, positive approach to running, which, as it is learned, can become a new approach to life as well.

CHAPTER TWO

RUNNING AND RELAXATION

THE SECRET TO TOTAL RUNNING IS RELAXATION. TO understand and derive benefit from the succeeding chapters, you must first understand the principles of *relaxed running*. Tension—in muscles, running style, breathing, and attitude —is the main reason people lose interest in running.

The importance of relaxation transcends running, of course. Frequently the lack of relaxation in our life-styles leads to the most common of diseases, physical as well as psychological (the most recent estimate is that three-fourths of all minor disease is psychosomatic in origin). Most people don't appreciate the need for relaxation, or know that it must be based on temperament and life-style. For instance, a harried executive, used to constant stress, may try to relax by lying for an hour on a sofa and not be relaxed at all; because of his personality, he may just become more restless and worried. Perhaps he needs an active form of relaxation.

Running itself can eventually become a form of relaxation. As a Harrisburg, Pennsylvania, runner wrote, "I find

I'm much more at ease and able since I started." Though some relaxation may come naturally, the principle of relaxed running must be deliberately striven for.

"Attempt to consciously relax," Thaddeus Kostrubala said. "If you aren't trained, you cannot do it, but if you are trained you can actually cause psychological effects."

Relaxation training is at the root of most of the recent self-help fads—for example, TM and *est*. Biofeedback, in particular, places a great importance on relaxation, and has been used to successfully conquer serious disease by teaching people that they can have mental control over their physical actions.

A better understanding of relaxation can give you a longer life. The longest-living people have understood the importance of being relaxed. Inhabitants of the Hunza Valley in Pakistan, renowned for extremely long lifetimes free of degenerative disease, sit in a completely relaxed state for fifteen minutes each day. This is a practice of TM; in fact, most M.D.'s recommend that at least fifteen minutes a day be devoted to a specific form of relaxation.

Relaxation can also retard our common tendency toward a lifetime of too much stress and too little body concern. A recent experiment at Columbia Presbyterian Medical Center involved six patients with severe peripheral vascular disease in a relaxation training program. When they started the program, the patients had been through two years of conventional treatment and could walk only two or three blocks at a time. After three months of relaxation training, each could walk a mile or more with no discomfort.

With the lack of attention to the importance of relaxation in our life-styles, it is natural that many people aren't able to relax while running. Those who report the break-throughs, who say running has transformed them, are the ones who have developed a unique sense of relaxation. Those who don't, who try running and say it's no fun, are those who never learned to relax.

Most runners reach a point beyond which running either becomes relaxation or becomes drudgery. If it becomes relaxation it can, like meditation, positively affect the runner's alertness and productivity. Such a state must be consciously developed, but is available to anyone who desires to learn it.

Brooklyn, New York, runner William D. says, "Running does relax me. It feels good to force my body to perform for a while each day. My mind sort of ranges over my experiences and I let go. I do spend some time, especially at the beginning of a run, thinking about running and concentrating on form and listening to my body's feelings and general condition. This rarely lasts more than fifteen minutes or so."

STYLE

The first step in becoming relaxed is examining your style. Some say the best style is the one that comes naturally. Unfortunately, this is not always so. It is wrong to think that running style is something that cannot be consciously altered or improved. A runner I ran with in high school demonstrated this very clearly. He decided to change his specialty from long-distance running to the half mile, and set out consciously to change his style from flat-footed to running on his toes. During a several-month off-season, he successfully trained himself to run on his toes and has run that way ever since, running faster times and becoming a more efficient competitive runner.

Improper style hampers many runners from ever becoming fully relaxed and discovering what running can do for them. A Carlisle, Pennsylvania, runner, Kevin C., said, "At first, I'll admit I had a horrible time at it. I'm lanky and I'd run leaning forward and I never seemed comfortable. I figured I was too thin for running, it just didn't come to me naturally at all. So then, after quitting several times, I started experimenting with different styles of running and I found one that was much better—I quit leaning forward (Arthur Lydiard told me this when I met him in 1977) and straightened up and I've liked running better ever since."

The essential principle of relaxed running is finding the style that wastes the least amount of energy. The following ideas contribute to this most economical, most relaxed running style:

Run erect. Ideally, the runner's upper body should be perpendicular to the running surface. The most common error is running with the pelvis and torso tilted forward; this puts undue strain on the legs, and can cause general fatigue as well as hamper efficient breathing.

According to former United States Olympic coach Bill Bowerman, position of the pelvis is the main basis of a proper running style. "A forward lean might be useful for someone trying to bash down a wall," Bowerman said. "But in running it merely gives the muscles a lot of unnecessary work."

Avoid over-long, or too-short stride. Overstriding is one

of the most common energy wasters. Similarly, a short, choppy stride simply tires the runner out too soon.

Land on the heels. Some runners naturally land on the balls of their feet; they walk and run this way and always have. Others naturally land on the heels. The latter style is advantageous when running distances longer than a half mile. Landing anywhere but on the rear of the foot causes unnecessary leg strain and may lead to shin splints. Optimally, the runner should land on the outer edge of his foot, toward the back.

Develop an economical rhythm of footfall. The lightest, quietest footfall is the most economical. When the foot lands, it should have already passed the farthest point of advance and be on its backswing. It should land directly below the knee, squarely beneath the runner's body. Toes should be pointed straight ahead.

Don't tense shoulders. There is a common tendency to raise or hunch the shoulders while running. This is an unnecessary action that tenses the entire running style. Shoulders also shouldn't roll uncontrollably; they should remain loose, but stable.

Carry arms low and relaxed. Two frequent mistakes in running style are carrying the arms too high and running with arms stiff and elbows "locked." Carrying the arms too high leads to a shortened stride and undue tension in the shoulders. The locked elbow produces muscle tension in the upper body. Arms should be loose, one arm swinging smoothly forward while the opposite leg advances.

Keep the face relaxed. Oddly, the head and facial muscles have a tremendous effect on the relaxation of the rest of the body. The most commonly overtensed facial muscles are those at the base of the neck and the lower jaw muscles. As running writer Joe Henderson says, "If good efficient style starts in the arms and torso, relaxed running begins in the head and shoulders."

A completely flawless running style doesn't exist, but most runners can become much more efficient and more relaxed. Examine your style for weaknesses and then work toward improving them, one at a time.

BREATHING

Eccentric Percy Cerutty, coach of world-record holders and of Olympic champion Herb Elliott, believed the key to progress in athletics was developing proper breathing techniques. His controversial galloping running movements were based on getting more oxygen into the lungs.

Cerutty's idea had a great deal of validity to it. Runners only utilize a small percentage of their lung space when they breathe—perhaps as little as 10 percent. Poor breathing also contributes to muscle tension, fatigue, and headaches.

As James Hewitt, author of *The Art of Relaxed Living*, wrote, "Civilized man has lost the art of breathing properly. His shallow breathing utilizes only about one-tenth of his lungs."

Part of becoming sufficiently relaxed is developing a deep rhythmic breathing pattern. This can be cultivated by practicing breathing exercises. After all, breathing is important not only in running but in all of life!

Belly Breathing. "Most of us breathe backwards," wrote

Jack Shepherd and Bob Glover in their *Runner's Handbook*. When we should be expanding the diaphragm, we restrict it by sucking in our stomachs. Practice expanding the belly as you inhale.

Rhythmic Breathing. Many runners deliberately incorporate a great deal of rhythm into their breathing; some do it naturally. "The idea," wrote Ian Jackson, in *Yoga and the Athlete*, "is to enter a rhythm of breathing corresponding to your physical movement." This is certainly a sound psychological technique. Cerutty employed a similar method, which he called Tidal Breathing. This involved having his athletes breathe in rhythm with the waves as they ran in the sand along the ocean. This puts the runner in a more relaxed, harmonious frame of mind.

The beginning runner, who is learning relaxation, should begin by inhaling and exhaling in a deliberate rhythm, paying close attention to each breath coming in and going out, using the belly breathing technique. Rhythmic breathing can also make the runner more aware of the process of his running and make him appreciate it more. The next step, then, is to breathe deeper and hold the breath for several seconds, first filling the abdomen and then the chest. Release the air from the chest first and then from the abdomen. If this breathing practice is done for several minutes at the beginning of each run, the rest of the run will be more relaxed.

Yoga Breathing. These breathing techniques are designed to give a greater bodily awareness and to create an overall relaxation:

1. *Pranayama.* Block the right nostril with your right thumb and breathe in deeply for five seconds; hold for

twenty seconds, cover the left nostril and exhale for ten seconds out of the right nostril. Repeat several times. Try this, albeit cautiously, while running.

2. *Sitkari.* Clench your teeth and inhale air through your mouth with a snakelike sound. Exhale through the nostrils.

3. *The Yoga Cleansing Breath.* Inhale deeply through the nose, then quickly pull in your stomach so that the air is forced back out through the nostrils. This should be done five to ten times at first and then eventually twenty times at once. Initially it might create a light-headed sensation. Stop when this occurs. It will disappear with practice.

Meditative Breathing. This will be discussed at greater length in Chapter Five; however, the most basic of the meditative breathing methods are relevant to learning beginning relaxation. With this type of breathing, the actual inhalation and exhalation matter less than concentration on that breathing. The Breath Count is a common exercise here. For the entire course of your run, count each breath that you exhale, up to ten. Once you reach ten, begin again. If you lose count, start over. This will strengthen concentration and will also make it easier to relax at will.

Joseph Goldstein wrote about this type of breathing in his book *The Experience of Insight: A Natural Unfolding,* saying:

> The breath may become erratic, fast or slow, fine or deep. Stay with it. One to ten. . . . It may be that after about five minutes, the mind starts thinking, "This is stupid, I'm not going to sit here for an hour and count to ten." Keep counting. And if, because of that thought you miss a breath, back

to one again. It may be that all kinds of tensions arise in the body. Ignore them. . . . This is a way to specifically strengthen the one-pointedness factor of mind, training it to stay on a single object.

Alternate Mouth and Nose Breathing. Many runners practice naturally inhaling from the nose and exhaling just from the mouth, and vice versa. This is mostly valuable as a rhythmic breathing exercise.

MENTAL RELAXATION

The mind must be relaxed for running to be relaxed. Mental relaxation may come naturally through some of the physical relaxation methods, but usually must be developed independently.

One of the primary means of becoming more relaxed mentally is being conscious of one's thought process while running. This is the basis of the meditation exercises in Chapter Five. Being conscious of one's thought process is also a means toward greater self-understanding. Thought Observation is the process of becoming consciously aware of all the thoughts that pass through your mind during a given space of time. Concentrate on the *procedure* of your thinking, on the method by which a thought enters your mind, and the way it leads to other thoughts. Notice how thoughts connect. Try to determine the roots of your thoughts. Allan H., a Davis, California, runner, explained how he employed this method: "I've used a number of meditation and Zen techniques in my running, and improvised somewhat too. I try to make it as introspective as possible. . . . Sometimes, I will focus my attention on the process of my thinking. Every thought that enters my head will be examined: Where did it come from? What was I thinking about just before that caused it to arise? It's fascinating to observe how our thoughts evolve. This is not only a valuable means of running, it is a supreme intellectual communication with self."

Another means of relaxing the mind is through Visualization, separating oneself from immediate surroundings and imagining oneself to be in a completely different environment. Some runners, including world-class marathoners such as Olympic Trials marathoner Jim Bowles, say they imagine themselves not only in a different environment, but even as a completely different person. One runner in the survey said she frequently pretends she is an animal, a horse, a deer, or an antelope.

In Visualization, concentrate on the first place that vividly comes to mind and, when that begins to fade, go to another.

John N., of Palo Alto, California, described how he goes through this process: "Occasionally, I'll drift so far from reality that I'll imagine I'm running in another part of the country. One time I convinced myself I was back in Delaware, which is where I grew up. One time I even convinced myself I was in the nineteen fifties. It's weird, but an interesting experience when it happens."

Visualization is difficult to do effectively, though it is hastened with regular practice. It is similar to the principle that is being used in Fort Worth, Texas, by Dr. Carl Simonton to treat cancer patients. Dr. Simonton theorizes that since mental and emotional factors may contribute to the formation of cancer, mental training can help offset those factors.

Ideally, Visualization, Thought Observation, and the other relaxation techniques should be practiced early in a run so the runner can develop the habit of becoming relaxed quickly.

Attitude. The effectiveness of any of these mental or physical relaxation techniques depends on a positive, creative, or at least open, attitude. Most runners have difficulty consistently putting their mind into a suitably calm state, slowing down their thoughts. Even with relaxed breathing and relaxed body movements, there must also be a relaxed attitude for complete relaxation to occur.

In *Your Body: Biofeedback at Its Best,* Beata Jencks wrote, "For stress prevention, relaxation of body and mind must be achieved, sufficient physical exercise and mental stimulation must be available."

Many runners say they deliberately cultivate a relaxed attitude immediately before beginning a run, by sitting quietly reading, listening to music, or just thinking. Others begin with a tense attitude and use running to relax. However, whether this occurs easily is an individual matter. Some observe that running while depressed doesn't make them any less depressed. Alexandria, Virginia, runner Dirk D. said, "Running's good except for one time: when I've got a real nasty mood. Then, the run'll just make me worse. When I'm in a real bad mood the best thing I can do is go lock myself in the bathroom."

Many with bad attitudes, though, don't give themselves a chance to change on a run; they tend to grind through the run, mind stuck in a groove of tense thought.

A very bad attitude *can* be relieved, if not removed, through running, but one must first know how to become mentally relaxed. Michael V., a Redding, California, runner, explained how he relaxed his attitude for running: "It's a meditative act for me to run and there's no way I can let myself go into it all tense and keyed up, worrying about things. That would be defeating my purpose. Running wouldn't be enjoyable if I let myself do that. So, even if I'm tense beforehand, I'll slow down for the run. I'll sit and get ready. I'll close off negative thoughts, I'll tell myself to relax, to put my mind on things that are less tense. I'll think about how nice it can be running outside in the fresh air if I let it be. And, by the time I'm ready to go, I've usually keyed down quite a bit. I'm ready to go, to enjoy the run, not just to get through it."

Eventually, with regular practice, such an attitude can become habitual.

GENERAL RELAXATION

There are dozens of relaxation techniques that can produce some of the same benefits as running, and that can aid running. These are supplements to running that can lead to a more relaxed life-style.

Yoga. Yoga has been used as a means of relaxation and enlightenment since 2000 B.C. Followers believe it can retard the aging process and prevent degenerative disease. Many runners do yoga before or after they run. Some say it has had profound effects on them.

Boulder, Colorado, runner John C. said, "Yoga played a big role in getting me sold on running." And Ian Jackson, in his book *Yoga and the Athlete*, wrote, "I might easily have become another stale running dropout. But yoga kept pushing me back."

Yoga is more than just an exercise: it is a religious commitment, a way of life. It is directly related to discipline, to the idea that by mental and physical self-discipline we can reach greater spiritual levels of consciousness. The yoga text, *Yoga Sara Sangrala*, gives this definition of yoga: "The silencing of the mind's activities which leads to the complete realization of the intrinsic nature of the Supreme Person is called Yoga."

More simply, yoga is the stretching of various muscle groups in a meditative fashion, holding one position for a length of time. One of the most basic of the yoga exercises is *Trataka*, which involves staring steadily, without blinking, at a candle flame until the eyes become teary. Besides improving concentration and eyesight, this exercise is often credited with enhancing one's powers for clairvoyancy. It is a good prelude to the meditation exercises in Chapter Five.

Yoga breathing, which is more than just a breathing practice, strengthens the abdominal muscles. The most fundamental is *Uddivana*, in which you stand in a slight crouch, leaning forward, with hands on knees. From this position, expel all the air from your lungs and, as you do so, suck in your stomach, pulling on the abdominal muscles as much as you can. Hold this position for ten seconds. Do several repetitions.

The follow-up exercise is *Nauli*, in which, after inhaling, you apply a pressure on the thighs with your hands. You should do this with one thigh at a time, and should be able to see, or at least feel, its effect on the abdominal muscles. As with all yoga exercises, there should be a concentration on the various parts of the body as you are doing the exercises. These breathing exercises have been credited with lessening stomach disorders and obesity.

One of the more common yoga positions is the *Posterior Stretch*, which resembles a sit-up. Begin lying flat on your back, then gradually sit up and try to touch your feet. Hold the toes and keep this position for ten seconds. Do ten repetitions. If you can't reach your toes, hold the position as far as you can reach. This can also be done standing up.

Another yoga position is the *shoulder stand*. Begin by lying on your back, legs together. Lift your legs from the floor and support your back until the legs are pointing upward, perpendicular to the floor. From here, point your toes upward toward the ceiling and hold for ten seconds. Repeat several times.

Two other positions are the *Bow Posture* and the *Cobra Posture*, in both of which you begin lying on your stomach. In the Bow Posture, lie flat and then stretch your arms back behind you. Bend your legs upward at the knee, and then reach back until you grab your ankles. Lift up your torso and pull your legs forward.

In the Cobra Position, lie flat on your stomach and lift just your upper body from the floor, as much as possible. Keeping your legs flat on the floor, lift your head and torso, so that you are looking toward the ceiling and your torso is as upright as possible. Try to hold this for ten seconds and repeat several times.

One final position, designed to afford the greatest degree of relaxation of any of the yoga exercises, is the *Corpse*

Posture. This should be done at the end of a yoga session. Some runners say they do it after they have completed their run. In this position, which aims to attain a total body relaxation, lie on the floor, completely still and relaxed. Remove any irritating clothing, and do it on a comfortable surface such as a soft carpet or a bed. Try to become as completely relaxed and unmoving as possible. Then, consciously attempt to relax all your muscles, gradually and in a designated order, working from the head down. Concentrate on relaxing the scalp muscles first, then move down the face. Although it may take a number of attempts before this posture brings great relaxation benefits and possibly weeks before it is fully mastered, it is the exercise that can have the greatest benefit.

Of course there are dozens of other yoga positions, which can be found in books specifically devoted to the subject. But together these exercises give the basic benefits of total relaxation, and begin the progression of Total Running. If done as a program, they can tone up all of the muscles, remove fat, improve the spine, posture, liver, kidneys, glands, and can have a positive effect on menstrual problems, asthma, obesity, insomnia, and varicose veins.

Hypnotism. Great interest has developed in the effects of hypnotism and autohypnotism (self-hypnosis) on running, both competitively and noncompetitively. Hypnotism has long been used in other areas besides running to relieve stress. More recently, runners have discovered the stress-removing benefits of hypnosis.

To reach a state of deep relaxation is the first step in self-hypnosis. This involves sitting in one spot with no noise and letting your mind clear; this, like the corpse yoga position, requires practice to master. It will be easier after the meditation exercises in Chapter Five are learned. As with the yoga and breathing exercises, you then strive to become completely relaxed, with no constricting clothing; close your eyes and take a series of deep breaths for several seconds to enhance the relaxed state. Then, begin to tell yourself over and over again what it is you want to hypnotize yourself to believe. According to a 1978 *Runner's World* article, we can easily hypnotize ourselves to become relaxed while running.

"Once you are completely relaxed and in the so-called 'trance,'" Richard Bourne, the author of the article, wrote,

> you can begin programming yourself for running. . . . I wouldn't recommend using self-hypnosis immediately before a run, because you need transition time between deep rest and physical exertion. Fifteen to thirty minutes is sufficient for the restful state of your body and mind to return to normal wakefulness. Each runner can devise a personal set of instructions. . . . After deep rest is attained, talk to yourself in a strong, commanding tone. Don't talk aloud, but subvocally; one part of your mind to another.

Bourne points out also that it is better, when talking to oneself, to use "you" in setting the commands, rather than "I."

Aaron J., an over-forty runner from Durham, North Carolina, who competed at the World Masters Championships in 1977, says he has frequently hypnotized himself before competition.

But hypnotism is better for relaxation than for competition, and it helps to first understand the ideas of breathing and yoga.

MASSAGE

Most people have areas of their body that are usually more tense than others, areas that most need relaxing. In fact, Reichian therapy theory states that our body build, posture, and muscle tension are all an extension of our personalities. A shy person, for instance, will tend to have a more curled posture than an overly confident person.

Massage is a more valuable means of relaxing individual parts of the body than other, more overall relaxation exercises. And, an overall relaxation can be cultivated through massage as well. Besides causing muscular relaxation, massage prevents muscle atrophy and increases the blood supply to joints. It is especially valuable in relaxing those afflicted with arthritis.

Some claim a special expertise is required to massage a person; others, more accurately, believe that anyone can effectively perform massage, with little or no practice.

Conflicting ideas about massage abound. Some believe it is a mild form of relaxation, while others say it can cure all human woes. In the book *Reflexology—It Works,* author Woody Dexter wrote that through muscle manipulation of the feet, *"immediate relief* is obtained from most ailments." He also claimed that "cancer is going to be knocked out by working on parts of the body known to Reflexologists."

Many chiropractors claim to be able to clear up any muscle tension in minutes. It's not necessary to go to a chiropractor, though, to obtain a relaxing massage. Some simple, very effective massage can be done by a friend.

For basic massage, move both hands in a smooth rhythm over the especially tense areas of a person's body. Ten to fifteen strokes a minute is advised. There are various ways in which massage can be done. Massaging with the fingertips is advised for tension in the joints (but be careful not to accidentally scratch the person's skin with your fingernails). Thumb massage is useful on the hands and feet. One-handed massage is best on the neck and the back of the head. Two-handed massage can also be useful on the neck and head, as well as on the back and chest.

If the discomfort is severe, the massager should try a deeper massage, pressing down into the skin, though without causing a painful reaction. Another means of massage is kneading, which means grabbing, lifting, and then deeply massaging muscle areas.

For all of the massage techniques, it is essential that a rhythm be maintained throughout if the person receiving the massage is to be properly relaxed. This can be accomplished by stroke rhythm or by circular massage.

ROLFING

Recently, a number of runners have turned to Rolfing and have found that their body is more relaxed and their running more enjoyable. Rolfing differs from chiropractic and some forms of massage in that it aims to develop an overall alignment and relaxation of the body, rather than just working on specific parts. Also known as Structural Integration, Rolfing is designed to put the body in a straight line, from head through spine to feet, by manually manipulating the muscles and connective tissues. More than just a physical therapy, it leads to many mental benefits, as do all of the relaxation techniques. According to Ida Rolf, originator of the concept, ". . . A great deal of emotional pains and aches disappear as well, because emotional pains and aches are usually anchored, so to speak, in problems of the physical flesh. The little hang-ups, our emotional hang-ups, are literally walled into that physical flesh. Before we can really get rid of them, we have to change the flesh and the relationships within it."

This is the philosophy of yoga and, like yoga, Rolfing requires strict commitment. As with TM, instruction is necessary. The benefits of Rolfing aren't dramatically different from those obtained through a thorough yoga program.

RUNNERS' IDEAS

Many runners ignore the more established means of relaxation and evolve their own. As Total Running progresses, you should learn and develop your own individual best relaxation program. To an extent, everyone has some natural means of relaxation. Here are three from the survey:

Kenny B., Santa Rosa, California: "The way I get tuned into running is with music. I always listen to some good rock music before I run and then get those songs going in my head. I also have a stereo headset that I run with sometimes. Running along the beach wearing that and having a Fleetwood Mac song come on—that's peaceful!"

Cindy M., Seattle, Washington: "I make up songs while I'm running; I do it all the time. If I get a good tune or a good line, I'll sort of keep repeating it over and over again. I guess it acts sort of like a mantra."

Nick A., Orlando, Florida: "I've got a weird approach to running. Right before I go out, I drink a sixteen-ounce can of Schlitz. I do this three or four times a week, partly because I run after work. When I'm done I feel good and relaxed."

RELAXATION AND THE SUBCONSCIOUS

Running's effect on overall relaxation is related to its subtle effects on our brain waves. According to Princeton's Lester Fehmi, brain-wave training is "a general, profound type of relaxation."

Although no one has determined the exact nature of the effect running has on brain waves, many runners say they are able to think more clearly, and say they have been able to better understand their subconscious mind.

Many find that relaxation surprises them with thoughts of genius and great personal insight. This is how genius operates: speed alone doesn't necessarily solve problems. Often, our subconscious needs to dwell on them.

As Claude Bristol wrote in *The Magic of Believing*, "Many great leaders, industrialists and inventors have openly declared that they have followed the hunches which have come to them in odd moments of relaxation or in periods when they were engaged in some other task than trying to solve their problems. A good way to let your subconscious mind solve a problem is for you to tackle it from all angles consciously; then, some night just before dropping off to sleep, order the subconscious mind to bring you the answer. . . . Be quick to grasp it when it comes and waste no time in following through with it."

When you try to force great thoughts, they usually don't occur, but when you become extremely relaxed and let your mind drift, you will sometimes surprisingly arrive at them.

"I'm often out jogging along real smooth and slow," said Patty K., of Los Angeles, "when I'll suddenly get some hot idea or figure out something that's stumped me for weeks. I'm always surprised by these moments. They seem magical sometimes."

Running first requires relaxation then it becomes relaxation itself. Once this happens, it can be used as an instrument of greater perception, yielding increased contentment and, eventually, increased success.

CHAPTER THREE

RUNNING AND CONTENTMENT

ONE OF THE SIMPLEST EFFECTS OF TOTAL RUNNING, which comes with relaxation, is that you become more content.

Personal problems and insecurities, though less verbalized than in the 1960's, have never been greater than they are today. Though diversions—sex and drugs, for instance—have become increasingly available for those seeking temporary contentment, true happiness is as elusive as ever. In fact, many people seem to be losing their conceptions of what happiness is.

Perhaps this is why runners frequently speak of "transformations." Many of these transformations are simply realizations of a long-repressed ability to be happy, or at least happier. In the survey, 56 percent said they generally are less depressed since they started running. Fifty-seven percent agreed that if they ran when depressed their depression was eased. "Running has been wonderful to me," said John O., of Baltimore, Maryland. "I'm no longer depressed."

But you don't have to be depressed for running to render positive effects. It can help carry anyone to new levels of contentment, based on greater self-understanding and confidence.

After practicing and developing the relaxation exercises, once again try running in the free-form manner described in the first chapter—run in an unfamiliar locale, with absolutely no goals of time and distance. Run as you feel. After developing the techniques of relaxation, this type of running should be more profound and interesting than when you first tried it.

The contentment running can add to people's lives is in part a result of the running "euphoria," but it goes beyond that. Running permits those lacking in self-confidence to see themselves accomplish something; it forces people to be alone with their thoughts, separates them from their work and obligations. It offers experiences of the mind, simple but profound, often never allowed in the rest of our existence.

William D., of Brooklyn, New York, said, "Running makes me feel better. It has given me greater confidence and insights into the workings and importance of my body."

Running, if approached in a rational, relaxed manner, as detailed in the previous chapter, may lead to a greater self-appreciation, and can be a crucial part of a program leading to contentment.

THE SEARCH FOR CONTENTMENT

Our current society has been characterized as one of quiet inner turmoil. The suicide, divorce, and alcoholism rates have all climbed. It's a repressive society, no less dangerous than the expressive and aggressive culture of the 1960's.

We're now more inclined to first try to understand our psyches before we tackle the world. An industry has suddenly grown up around relaxation and self-help programs. We relax to recover, as deliberately as a sufferer of a nervous breakdown might, in his attempt to adjust to the world of sanity.

After the initial social changes of the 1960's, we have a massive, subtle culture shock, a nervous breakdown en masse. Many are still trying, subconsciously, to make sense of the changes that occurred in the 1960's and the effect of those changes on them. Much of Alvin Toffler's *Future Shock* philosophy has come true sooner than expected.

In this context, something as meditative as running becomes particularly relevant, helping to reintegrate us with progressive thinking and delivering us from the alienation of change.

"I was much more depressed before I started running," said Michael N., of Santa Cruz, California. "I was having more problems worrying about things, coping with things, people, and then after I started running I worried about it less and it went away a little."

Almost everyone could be happier. Even those who think they are well off aren't without lingering doubts and submerged fears. With running, there is usually an obvious physical improvement, a mental reaction—of confidence and well-being—to that improvement, and usually a more active approach to one's life. You become more confident about your physical appearance, feel more able and uniformly satisfied as you see yourself steadily progress, not just in physical ability but in your ability to derive mental benefits from the free-form approach to running. Finding subtle, regular pleasure from running is a steady progression of being properly relaxed, experimenting, and running without goals.

THE INDIVIDUAL EXPERIMENT

First in importance in developing Total Running is relaxation, discussed in the previous chapter. Also essential are location and schedule. Some people are better suited to running in the morning, others prefer to run in the evening. The best rule is that if you're not fully enjoying running, if it seems to be adding to rather than removing some of your tension or discontent, then you should change your running. Experiment; find what is most comfortable. By practicing what feels most natural you should evolve to the point where you never go to a run with a feeling of obligation.

If you frequently look at your run with negative thoughts and dread the idea of sweating under a hot sun, you probably need a new approach.

PROPER APPROACH

Here is a specific example of how running can become an aid to contentment, offered by San Francisco runner Annie W., who began running more than six years ago, but went through several trials before finally being able to enjoy it.

"I was working as a legal secretary when I first came out here from Massachusetts. I needed exercise because I was drinking some wine each evening and was getting a little flab about my waist. So I'd go to the marina green each day and do two or three laps. But it was a pain, just another thing that I had to do, there was nothing special about it."

It was about this time that Annie read several accounts about the "running high"; she reacted with confusion. There was nothing transcendent about running the oval of San Francisco's marina green. In fact, it became boring very quickly.

"I got into a situation where every little crack in the earth, every anthill, became ingrained into my memory and it was just simply boring seeing that same anthill three times each day. It didn't occur to me then that I should change my course; I saw all these other people running in circles and I figured that's what jogging was all about."

Did running have any effect, then, on her well-being? "Sure, but nothing positive. I'd hate going out there. It would take me three-fourths of the run before I became relaxed. And at this point, I was still fairly new to San Francisco and didn't have a whole lot of friends; I imagined that I'd meet some joggers. Actually, as I look at it now, my first running experiences were nothing but disillusionment. I didn't enjoy it and I didn't meet anyone else."

As many people who hear of the "running high" do, she quit when it didn't magically materialize. She didn't realize that the problem wasn't running at all, just her approach to running. Six months later, a fellow worker asked Annie to join in a noontime run around the company park. It affected her right away.

"Running had sort of drifted out of my mind. It just stopped being relevant to me. Then, a girlfriend asked me if I'd be interested in going out one noontime on a run. I agreed, somewhat reluctantly. I had all these visions about the last time, on the marina, about how lonely and unpleasant that had been. But this was something entirely different. We ran around the park and it was cool and we had a great talk and I just felt amazingly *refreshed* by the whole thing."

Within a month Annie was again running regularly herself, jogging slowly each evening in the suburban streets by her home. It amazed her.

"The source of my exhilaration was surprise, I think: It was so completely different from before. I'm glad I stumbled on it again. I'm much more pleased with my life, my attitude to others, everything; it's beautiful."

It wasn't a permanent enjoyment, though: there were still several transformations in store. About a year after running had seemed such a source of bliss, she was promoted to office manager, was given more responsibility, frequently had to work later; her whole attitude shifted.

"I became a bit more restless, I guess. I began drinking more in the evening. I looked forward to the drink all of a sudden more than the run. That was my problem. Finally, one day I just said, 'Hey, I'm not enjoying this running, why am I doing it?' I quit again, for about four months."

She says now that the four months were important in crystallizing an understanding of what she was doing. Finally, she felt so much tension, she changed her job voluntarily.

"The day I switched I went on a run and it all came

back; I mean everything clicked. I was in another world. It felt so good and so right. I thought right then that I would never again quit running, and I haven't since."

Today, Annie enjoys running as much as ever. She simply had to work out for herself how running could be enjoyable in the context of her own life-style. It took experimentation before running fit in naturally. For most people it happens sooner; for some, it's just a matter of weeks. As in Annie's case, contentment comes when running is an integral part of your way of life, when you don't force yourself to run but let Total Running find you.

THE PSYCHOLOGY OF CONTENTMENT

"I realized I didn't need to have negative thoughts if I didn't want to," said upstate New York runner Mrs. Myrna P. It took running to bring that realization to her.

We all possess that same power, not to be discontent. But our tendency is never to make or allow ourselves to consciously realize this. We are inclined to passively let our happiness slide away as things begin to go wrong. But we don't have to accept the momentum of the slide.

A friend of mine recently explained how she had come to be less depressed and more optimistic. "I just told myself 'no' whenever it would start to happen. As soon as I'd start to get depressed I'd force myself to think about something else, something positive, or I'd go out and do something. I just don't dwell on it and the depression really seems to go away."

If we make such an effort, it can eventually become habitual and we can learn to avoid depression for good.

Oddly, we usually know what is making us unhappy but we don't try to give up our depression.

Some depression is probably valuable in that it leads to change, but the same process can come through a contented life-style that includes some self-evaluation.

We need to jump into our depression, come out, and wipe off the negative influences. "He has half the deed done who has made a beginning," wrote Horace. Taking the initiative prevents the depression from sneaking up as a subtly rising tide while we suddenly find ourselves near drowning. We can learn to better understand depression and almost to deflect it at will.

In the survey, 57 percent of the runners queried said that they felt better afterward if they ran when depressed. This is the great value of running: it allows an opportunity to reflect on the cause of the depression and devise a way out. Other means of diverting depression—eating, drinking, going for a drive—aren't as effective because they aren't accomplishments. A runner combats depression even while contemplating it; a run is something positive, an accomplishment. On a run, worry often dissolves.

I've run several times while depressed. I remember once running by the beach, feeling oddly lethargic, dissatisfied with the work I was doing, feeling I was wasting so much time. Everything seemed wrong. It had been a struggle to convince myself to get out to run, and at first I felt heavy and very uncomfortable. But I changed. Seeing the people relaxing on the beach told me to settle down, to relax myself. I saw other runners, and began to feel better. The running felt right and powerful. There was nothing theoretical about it; rather, it was physical, and it produced a strong, clear emotion. I speeded up, seemed to be gliding, feeling a rare strong sense of power, of importance, a positive feeling.

Many runners report being wrenched from depressions by similar, essentially unexplainable sensations. Carla T., a Detroit, Michigan, runner, wrote, "Sometimes, I just experience this incredible gladness while I'm running. I just feel amazingly happy to be alive and able to run. It doesn't last real long but it's so powerful I get goose bumps."

This extreme alteration of emotions often completely wipes out negative thoughts that had seemed so troublesome before; it's the spark that is so hard to create. Of course, you won't have this profound experience each time you go out to run, but the change of environment and the active movement, the accomplishment of this physical activity, are positive mental influences on a negative attitude.

Total Running is an evolving discovery, approached with no preconceptions. The contentment it adds to your life may not always be in the form of tremendous euphoria, but may be in a subtle satisfaction. This differs with everyone. As New York City runner Marvin S. said, "I first expected a halo to form around my head and I'd turn into Dr. Sheehan or something. But nothing happened. I just got hot and started sweating. But you know, I'm glad for it. I don't think I could handle having to hold a conversation with the gods each time I decided to take a four-mile jog through Central Park."

HOW MUCH, WHEN, AND WHERE

Most running books include sample schedules and recommendations for an ideal day-by-day running program, including how many miles to run each week. Unfortunately, these programs, which completely ignore the runners' mental makeup, have a tendency to become dull quickly. There are no formulas for running. Whatever fits in most comfortably with your life-style is the ideal program for you. It will take a bit of experimentation to find the proper approach.

ASSOCIATION VERSUS DISSOCIATION

What do you think about while running? One runner in the survey said he figures out math problems; another said, "I just completely clear my mind of all thought."

In the meditation and Zen sections, there is a discussion of how to direct your thinking for the optimum benefits. But for beginners, who haven't yet evolved to that point, what to think about might sometimes be a problem.

A controversy has developed over whether a runner should purposely let his mind "spin out" (dissociate) or whether he should specifically try to concentrate on something (associate). Although you can consciously strive for either state, in general one or the other will occur naturally when you are properly relaxed, and often there will be a combination of both. There will be days when a specific problem will occupy the runner's mind and other days when his mind will wander.

Don Kardong, the 1976 Olympic marathoner, said that even in a world-class competition, he lets his mind wander for the first half of the race and daydreams. An extreme example of this dissociation was mentioned by Dr. William Morgan in a recent article in *Psychology Today* in which he recounted the story of a runner who had become so completely detached from a race that he imagined he saw a television set in front of him with himself running on the screen. He couldn't feel his feet hitting the ground and set a school record for that run. This feeling is similar to the euphoria many noncompetitive runners say they experience. But whether you will have such a run on any given day is something that—so far, at least—can't be predicted.

As Dr. Morgan wrote in that *Psychology Today* article:

Distance running is associated with lowered levels of anxiety and depression, two major problems of modern society; many psychiatrists and psychologists have recently described the efficacy of managing anxiety states and depression by means of jogging programs. . . . Dissociation appears to be far more pleasant, since it reduces anxiety, effort, [and] sense and general discomfort. On the other hand, the jogger who adopts it is more likely to suffer serious injury. The increased likelihood of stress fracture to the bones of the feet and lower legs cannot be ignored. The very real potential for heat stroke or heat exhaustion can lead to death or permanent impairment unless medical assistance is readily available. Finally, the beginning jogger should be warned that the quest for a "breakthrough" to "transcendent experience" can produce addiction and psychological traumas.

The extreme consequences Morgan mentions aren't likely to affect a recreational runner. The best advice is to try both approaches. Consciously think about a specific matter or the act of running one day and let your mind spin free other days. Probably it won't occur that completely: you'll find yourself doing a bit of both on most runs as you discover what comes most naturally to you.

THE STEPS TO CONTENTMENT

Self-therapy, which Drs. Greist and Kostrubala credit running with fostering, is the initial step in producing a more content life-style. You learn the errors of your habits through this and can ask yourself, "What are the barriers to contentment?" and then, "How can I remove them?"

As Beata Jencks wrote, in *Your Body: Biofeedback at Its Best*, "To modify voluntarily one's behavior, physiological activity, emotions, and mental processes by self-regulation is frequently possible. Often a person must learn to change his habits, but this can be done without instruments and great expense."

Most of us never fully accept the nature of our own personality, never form full opinions, never determine true motivation; we go through life, make friends, create families, but distract ourselves from the question of our own identity. Like Camus's character, we become simply strangers.

Running often acts as a catalyst, showing us what we truly desire, what the major barriers of habit are that cause lack of fulfillment. Running introduces us to our strengths and weaknesses. And, from this knowledge, it gives us the ability to eliminate the weaknesses and create more strengths. It allows us to realize our own standards and not be intimidated by others'.

Candy P., a runner from Portland, Oregon, summed up much of what happens to the person who approaches running properly: "I like myself better now. Running has given me a feeling of accomplishment and has taught me my limits, both mental and physical. Do I give up easily? Do I cancel my workouts when I'm depressed or don't feel like it? Also, through running, I've met different kinds of people and that has taught me more about how I interact with others."

The first step is this inner exploration. From it follows three other steps: deciding what needs to be changed, determining a plan to make the changes, and then carrying out the plan. Running can figure in each step. It is a thinking period in which ideas may coalesce to help you carry out your newly determined goals.

CHANGE

Stagnation is a temptation of such subtle degrees that we often recognize it only long after it has taken hold. The most obvious sign is the uncomfortable feeling of "going through the motions," doing things that once brought great joy and enthusiasm, but that have disintegrated to boring routines. These feelings often drift into a cynical attitude about all of life and cause us to stay away from any attempt to realize our potential. Often the feelings lead to disillusionment.

Usually, a change in life-style will bring back the enthusiasm. Of course, it takes an effort to make the change, but it's a worthwhile effort.

The success of the relationship between your running and your well-being will depend on change. If you jog each day around the local high-school track and get the feeling of "going through the motions" fairly regularly, running isn't doing much for you, almost nothing in relation to what it could do. You should use this as a cue that it's past time to change your running course, distance, or partners, and to work on your attitude.

If running feels like an obligation, either change it or don't do it at all. Once you see enthusiasm return through a change in your running, you'll develop a greater appreciation for change in your life-style and in your work as well.

Del B., a Pasadena, California, runner, illustrated this principle. "I stumbled into running almost by accident, it now seems. I never liked that clean sweatband and white socks look much. I certainly never wanted to be associated with that herd, let alone join it. I still don't particularly relate to all those joggers with their fashions and their wearing their jogging clothes in the grocery store. But once I did get into it, I suddenly said, 'What's going on? I like this.' I wondered what had seemed so repulsive about it before and if my old self would be repulsed seeing my new self out there with them all. And I found out that what had repulsed me was just the idea of change."

UNREASONABLE GOALS

Running is a simplifying activity. Any therapist will tell you that the best means of unscrambling a confused mind is through simplification. Confusion clears in a simplified environment. If we look at the various causes of unfulfilling life-style, certainly one of the more common difficulties is that of setting unreasonable goals and then finding disillusionment. Running, because of its simplicity, often lets people practice setting reasonable goals. The natural, simple aspect of running doesn't hamper great goals, but allows a better conception of them, of whether they are reasonable or merely dream-wishes.

A California actor and runner who spent several years scurrying about Hollywood trying to be a star, feeling depressed almost constantly, used running for just this purpose.

"I think I was most despondent," he wrote, "because I felt I was sacrificing so much, including my physical health, to be this great star and then it just wasn't happening. I'd get a few things, I did a couple of commercials, but no one seemed really interested."

He was then drinking heavily, eating poorly, and always short of money. Running, he says, did much to change his viewpoint.

"I got in shape and my priorities changed. Unreasonable goals aren't worth pursuing, I'll tell you. They aren't worth giving up your health for. If it happens, it happens. I mean fame and all of that. But just desire alone isn't going to get you there. Not even talent will. It's a tricky business and you've got to meet the right people for anything to happen, that's all. I'm not oriented that way anymore, mostly because I discovered that I care more about my health. And I feel a lot better now, too."

He admits his attitude was considerably different before he began running.

"For more years than I want to remember, I wanted to feel that aura of fame more than just about anything else. I scrimped and scrounged just to be around it. I don't even know, looking back, if I wanted to be famous, or if that scared me. I wasn't really sure. I'd seen people who were famous and I saw that if they believed they were responsible for it, then that fame controlled every single action they took at every single moment of their lives."

His uncertainty about his goals was cleared up through an evaluation brought about, in part at least, by running. This reassessment isn't necessarily deflating; you can still see great possibilities, but now you can distinguish them from unreasonable ones.

MASKS

As we saw in the previous example, running relates to contentment in that it lets us see our real selves, not images created by our imaginations and fears. The joy of running is the removal of guises, beginning with our own. "We wear the mask that grins and lies," wrote the poet Paul Laurence Dunbar. Self-knowledge, which leads to contentment, is what the runner strives for.

"I run because I like it," is the simplest description of the activity, offered by a Louisville, Kentucky, runner. "It makes me feel good and it makes me a better human being."

CHAPTER FOUR

RUNNING AND SUCCESS

SUCCESS, THOUGH EVERYONE DEFINES IT DIFFERENTLY, IS a universal desire. In fact, since it often translates to happiness, success might be said in one sense to be our primary desire.

What is success? Some see it as an evil obtained mostly through unscrupulous means. Others romanticize success, make it mystical, unobtainable (as Emily Dickinson wrote, "Success is counted sweetest/By those who ne'er succeed.").

These interpretations give success insufficient priority in our lives. We often don't consider that success is actually a simple realization of potential that might lead to greater happiness. A dictionary definition of success is "achieving desires or goals." This is what success means in this chapter. Obviously it is not the same as fame or splendor.

Previously, we have discussed how running can assist in the formation of a more relaxed and content life-style. Can it also create a more successful one?

This question arose recently on a noontime run I took

71

with a co-worker at the publishing house where I was employed. He explained the profound effects running had had on his life. Just months earlier, he had been uncertain of his goals, unconfident of his ability to carry any of them out, and generally dissatisfied with his life-style. His marriage was faltering and he admitted he was "screwing around in most areas" of his life. Finally, he forced himself to make a decision.

"I had to ask myself, 'Do I want to be a success or do I just want to mess around and be miserable the rest of my life?' "

His decision was to put his potential to use, to see how far it could take him. He credits two things with allowing him to carry out that decision: *est* and running. Of the latter he says, "Running relaxed me. It made me think more clearly. It really made me more aware of my life."

He quickly transformed his decision into action, making a conscious attempt to remove all of the negative influences in his life. He took a much more lucrative advertising job with a California publisher. He has since become not only more successful, but considerably more satisfied.

This account indicates how profound the link can be between running and success, particularly for those who are new to running. The reason, quite simply, is that running can remove many of the factors that commonly combine to produce a *lack* of success: feelings of inferiority and uncertainty, fear of failure, and depression. Running can break down these obstructions in very simple, often subtle ways. Although it may only occupy a small fraction of one's waking hours (a half-hour run is approximately 3 percent of the waking time of our day), running can lead to a more positive attitude throughout the rest of the day.

Maintaining and realizing a drive for success demands a consistently positive attitude, and this is where running becomes relevant. "It regularly livens my spirits," was the explanation offered by Joseph L., a runner from Allison, Iowa.

Runners discover keys to long-locked doors by being actively alone.

Said a runner from White Plains, New York, "I went to work each morning, waited for the coffee break, went to lunch, went home again at night, ate dinner, watched television, and went to sleep. Of course, I thought about a lot of other things, but I had convinced myself I was in a rut, and therefore I was.

"I no longer think that way, and I believe running has had a lot to do with my new attitude. I now run when I get home from work and it makes me look forward to my evenings more. It adds a great plus to my day. I approach work with a much better attitude too. I no longer think of it as just a space between coffee breaks and I'm accomplishing a lot more because of this."

THE NATURE OF SUCCESS

Success is the great American road sign: we all strive to be traveling toward it, we all enjoy the confidence of believing it is within our grasp. And yet despite sometimes meticulous mapping and plotting, few of us ever actually see our conceptions of success actualized. But how we love to try: people have killed, stolen, casually ruined others' careers in search of the always elusive Big Success. For some, the compulsive quest for success leads ultimately to self-destruction.

The obsession with success is not without irony: although most Americans desire it, few have taken the time to determine exactly what the thing is. It is this factor that prevents many from ever reaching success. Success for many is some vague entity that they aim for blindly, not knowing what it is, but feeling certain they will recognize it when they stumble upon it. Some take this vague idea with them to the grave.

Because of the tendency to associate great success with paradise, perfection, or, more commonly, money, there is a frequent inclination not to approach it with a realistic attitude or with the specific goals that could in fact lead us toward it.

A true attempt at success requires three elements: reasonable, flexible goals; a plan to accomplish those goals; and the ability and desire to carry out the plan.

This obviously requires a sense of ordered, though still intuitive and creative, thinking, which many say running helps to develop.

Three examples from the survey follow:

Ken B., Rochester, New York: "My work at school is better now, mainly because I'm more organized about it. I just do it more regularly. Running has helped me to schedule my life. That's probably the best thing it's done for me."

Karen W., Honolulu, Hawaii: "What has running done to me? It's made me rational, I guess."

Pat W., Columbus, Georgia: "It's peculiar, but my work just naturally became more systematic after I began running. Work and running complement each other wonderfully, I think. The anxieties are erased, and there seems to be an interesting interaction between the conscious and the subconscious that not only makes the work easier to get involved in but also there seems to be this amazing ability during the interaction for my mind to work out job-related problems almost subliminally."

This is an often-ignored part of success, the interaction between the parts of the mind. Success is, after all, more than just taking action; it is finding an effective balance in action and thought.

Perhaps the most basic definition of success is the development and utilization of one's potential through specific personal achievements. Thomas Wolfe, the robust American novelist, described it thus:

> If a man has a talent and cannot use it, he has failed. If he has a talent and uses only half of it, he has partly failed. If he has a talent and learns somehow to use the whole of it, he has gloriously succeeded and won a satisfaction and a triumph few men ever know.

This is because true success, though rare, carries with it true happiness; a partial success doesn't, nor does a rationalized success, which is no success at all.

THE INTUITIVE MIND

Generally, if a desire for success is implanted in the conscious mind, the subconscious will work on realizing it; an aid to this process is a regular "spin out" period (running writer Joe Henderson's description of running) in which the subconscious is allowed to roam at will.

In *The Subconscious Mind*, authors Erna Farrell Grabe and Paul C. Ferrell wrote, "There is dormant in each human being a faculty, whether it is developed or not, which will enable that particular individual to succeed if the *desire* for success is present in the conscious mind."

Running participates in and may even initiate the development of this faculty for success. The process leads to what one runner described as a "wholeness of thought." Running makes possible a successful interaction between the conscious and the subconscious. Few realize that they can develop the intuitive part of the brain through running, and that this development can have a positive impact on the realization of success.

It is cynicism that often prevents the full development of the mind. Locked into the routines of daily lives, many of us never consider our subconscious. We never learn to use the more intuitive parts of our minds. This is why the discovery of the insights of running is often such a profound experience. It invites runners into unrecognized portions of their mind and their potential. Total Running does this in an evolutionary fashion; a rapport develops with the inner self. People suddenly break through the dictates of their conscious mind, the preconceptions they had held for so long.

Claude M. Bristol wrote of this in his book, *The Magic of Believing*:

> Every student of the subject knows what may be accomplished by getting into direct contact with the subconscious mind—thousands have employed it to achieve wealth, power, and fame in this world as well as to cure physical ailments and solve countless human problems.

Gustave Geley, the French psychologist, said something similar—that the best achievements in life come from a harmony and cooperation between the conscious and the subconscious.

This is certainly something many runners come to know. One, Steven D., of Reno, Nevada, wrote, "I'm much fuller, my personality has assumed unsuspected dimensions. Some runs are still slow to please, sure, but on the other hand, some are so powerful that I get to look at who I really am but never bothered to see. I'm a better person all around for it."

ATTITUDE

Runners usually experience a noticeable strengthening of self-concept. Many suggest that the reason for this is simply that running is itself an achievement and it gives runners a more positive attitude about achievement in other spheres of their life. Those runners new to the benefits of running are among the most enthusiastic and creative of workers. "My drive in running carried right over into my work," said Oregon runner Bonnie F.

Attitude alone is often the greatest obstacle to achievement and success. When motivation ebbs and depression sets in, the fear of inability creeps in as well. This only carries us farther from our true abilities and potential.

Sandra K., a writer for UPI based in New York City, discovered running at a point when she was seeking employment. It benefited her greatly, by creating a much-needed positive attitude.

"Job hunting could have been a real hassle," she said,

"but instead became a challenge that I didn't mind, all because of running. . . . By being outdoors, and getting that 'high' feeling on completing a few miles, I developed an entirely different attitude about the frigid weather. Nothing seemed impossible. I would job-hunt on the coldest days, rarely feeling depressed because of the good feelings I carried over from running. As a writer, I now use jogging to iron out problems in my work. When I come across a writing obstacle, I go out and jog a few miles and always solve the problem by the time I'm back."

Ideas tend to jell during running and most people end their runs with considerably more enthusiasm and creative energy than when they began. Stubborn ideas become animated, sprout wings, take flight. As relaxed running is developed this can happen with regularity.

EVALUATION

"Introspective" is a word often used in describing running. "I learn a great deal about myself and my motivation by being alone on a quiet run," wrote Tom D. of Philadelphia. "I learn not to accept other people's ideas all the time and I learn what my own ideas really are."

This self-evaluation process is intimately related to achievement, because it allows people to be who they really are. Success depends not only on self-assurance, but often on self-knowledge.

André Gide wrote, "What another would have done as well as you, do not do it. What another would have said as well as you, do not say it; written as well, do not write it.

Be faithful to that which exists nowhere but in yourself—
and thus make yourself indispensable."

This, then, is the "secret" of success and the secret of
how running relates to success. It isn't uncommon for us
to be tripped by lack of self-knowledge and self-confidence
while aiming for success. Runners, though, generally report
a better self-understanding.

KNOWLEDGEABLE VERSUS SMART

Finding a path through opposing ideas is essential in
realizing success, as well as in just being content and self-
assured. F. Scott Fitzgerald defined intelligence as the
ability to keep two opposing ideas in mind at the same
time. But to move forward, to be successful, one needs to
find a true personal path through opposing ideas. This is
the distinction between being smart and being knowledgeable. Smart is being able to use one's knowledge. Many
very knowledgeable people aren't successful, or content,
because they aren't smart.

One survey respondent, a circulation director of a Los
Angeles magazine and mother of three, described her interpretation of this: "In the past, reading was the major
catharsis for my ideas. It was the most enriching means I
knew of understanding myself, my family, my social and
work acquaintances. This was the period when I would
explore myself. Running, now, has completed the catharsis,
it has made my thinking process much more refined. I now
run after reading and most frequently experience profound
realizations, bold new ideas. I get an initial explosion of
ideas from reading and the running gives me a truer inter-

pretation of them. It's wonderful. I wouldn't say it is the running itself so much as the fact that it follows reading. If you're dealing with a number of opposing ideas, running can give you a straighter interpretation; running can let you find your way through your ideas."

THE DEPRESSION BARRIER

A major impediment to being smart instead of just knowledgeable is depression; this can often come along unexpectedly and destroy plans and resolutions. The studies of Dr. John Greist at the University of Wisconsin and of Dr. Thaddeus Kostrubala at San Diego have shown that running can effectively and consistently relieve depression. Of course, it will probably take a bit of experimentation to apply this finding to individual people.

Some people don't actualize their success drives because they do too much of the wrong type of work and aren't able to relax sufficiently and enjoy what they are doing. For instance, Michael Lutz, lead guitarist with the rock group Brownsville Station, which has had several million-selling records, credits running with clearing negativity from his mind and giving him a better career perspective.

"In the early days," Lutz recalls, "we were just touring all the time and I never had the chance to sit down and figure out where I was going. My idea of bliss now is to run twenty miles in the morning, then play a gig at Madison Square Garden that evening."

Similarly, John W., of Aurora, Colorado, said that *not* running interferes with the success of his job by making him take it too seriously. "I used to get depressed a great deal," he said, "and a lot of the reason was the work. I was overworking and never finding time to relax. When I started jogging, I was much happier, and more relaxed and efficient at work. Now, if I miss more than a day or two of running, that depression comes back and I feel very tense."

For several years now, San Diego psychiatrist Thaddeus Kostrubala has been practicing what he refers to as "running therapy." By early 1978, he had introduced fifty-three patients to this novel therapy. He has found that, generally, after thirty minutes, patients let their inner barriers fall and suddenly are able to express themselves and, perhaps most significantly, see ways out of their problems. Many of his patients became marathon runners and most became more productive in other areas of their lives.

One of the most remarkable success stories was a twenty-year-old acute paranoid who was going to doctors nearly every day complaining of illnesses that existed only in his mind. Formerly an A student, his grades had dropped to Ds and Fs. After six months of running therapy, though, his paranoia was cured, his grades were As and Bs again—and he was running marathons.

Running acts to overcome negative thoughts and, as they are removed, success becomes more accessible.

THE HABIT OF SUCCESS

Success is a habit, but not one we learn simply; rather, we learn a series of habits, and these intricately combine to determine our success or failure.

The habits running creates are probably less important than the ones it dissolves. Many runners lose addictive tendencies. Dr. Kostrubala, for one, admits that before he started running he owned a deadly set of bad habits: severely overweight, he ate too much; he was an alcoholic; and he was unable to stay married.

Running can be so profound in aiming people on paths to success because it changes more than just isolated individual habits; it alters whole clumps of habits, almost automatically. Trying to change habits individually is often only frustrating, because, even if the change is successful, there is a good chance that equally negative substitute habits will have been created.

A Santa Barbara, California, housewife, Robin G., explains, "I don't think it's overly dramatic to say that I was once living in a trap. I realize it a lot better now, though, than I did then. I had become dependent on enough things to fill up my days and get me to sleep. Everything was an addiction. I watched the same television shows each day, drank two beers for lunch, cleaned up the kitchen before my husband got home, fixed dinner; I stared at the living-room rug a lot. Nothing changed and I guess nothing really happened. My life had become a cliché.

"Now I'm not going to say that running miraculously made me happy all the time (that's becoming a cliché too!) because it didn't. But once I started running, I began to change the way I do things. I gave up some of the TV shows and my two-beer lunch. I broke out of that cycle—something I'd tried unsuccessfully to do before. I saw that I didn't need those habits and then realized they weren't important or even enjoyable. I'm doing much more with my life now. I enjoy the outdoors, sports, and reading more."

It isn't the running itself so much as the resultant change

in habits and attitude that is so important and directly related to success.

THE RUNNING SPARK

Often the difference between success and lack of success is very slight. There is frequently some subconscious reason preventing success. Through the self-examination of running and the confidence of achievement, this preventing factor may be suddenly transcended.

That running can be intimately related to work was explained by Harry D., an Illinois physician and runner, who wrote me, "There are three main positive effects of running: 1) a pleasurable mental sensation of well-being; 2) an energizing effect; work and goal-seeking preparedness; 3) a mental sense of positive accomplishment of work and duty for contributing to one's well-being and for being able to better carry on one's work."

Kostrubala's studies seem to support this idea, that running can make people more positively productive. Probably any form of exercise can be employed as an aid to success if approached properly. Once the runner finds his rhythm and running becomes effectively integrated into his life-style, it will orient his life more toward productivity. It can serve as a spark that makes a whole life-style more positive.

THE LURE OF DISTRACTION

Unfortunately, the lure of distraction does many people in long before they ever come close to realizing their potential. We make far more resolutions than we ever carry out. Instead of acting on our desires, we are far more prone to analyze them, until we've found a rationalization for not acting, and then we don't have to pursue them at all.

Distractions, like stress, can be useful if they occur in moderation but, also like stressors, aren't usually experienced in moderation. Few recognize in themselves the absurdity of not removing some of their distractions for just a year or even months or weeks to see what their unobstructed potential might be.

One effect of Total Running is to make us aware of how distracting our life-style is. This will become especially clear through the meditation exercises in Chapter Five. Consider this statement from a Portland, Oregon, runner: "All that time alone on the roads made me test myself. I'd set up imaginary conversations sometimes. I'd even have interviews with myself. It might sound stupid but I learned a lot, especially what I really wanted to do with myself. But the first thing I learned was just that I was somewhat wasting my life, that I just wasn't doing all I could have been."

There is a clear distinction between distraction and relaxation. Relaxation is a pause with purpose, whereas distraction is disruptive. Distractions create anxiety and worry. They splinter concentration and goal achievement. Relaxation relieves anxiety, affords a release from pressure.

Relaxation is a necessary part of any drive for success, and of a fulfilling life-style. Distractions cause lack of achievement and fear; they pull success away from one's grasp. As Claude Bristol wrote in *The Magic of Believing*, "Success is a matter of never-ceasing application. You must forever work at it diligently. Otherwise, it takes wings and flies away."

RUNNING AND SUCCESS

Can running itself be a distraction? One survey respondent wrote, "At first, running was something I liked a little too much. I was so busy running and racing, I let my work slip."

Running can be used to make the rest of one's life productive, but if the running itself becomes the center of one's life, rather than a supplement, the other areas will very likely suffer. Then one will probably not be as content or productive as one could be.

POTENTIAL FOR SUCCESS

Potential for success varies greatly and is dependent on how successful a person already considers himself. Ask yourself how successful you feel. Contemplate it on the run. Know where you are before you decide where you want to go. A practical means of figuring success potential is by making a list of what goals you have set for yourself, small and large, and what the results have been. Then examine what, in each case, was the cause of your success or failure to meet these goals. Write down all this and then look for common denominators—you will find the most frequent barriers and distractions. You then know what to remove. Think all this out on the run and write it out afterward; it's the simplest success formula and therapy there is.

AN EXAMPLE

Often running lets us know we have a chance. Some, such as Dr. George Sheehan, call it the dividing point in their life. After their discovery of it, their thinking becomes more positive. But exactly how does running relate to success? The following case, which is somewhat typical, was offered me by one of those polled, whose life has completely changed through running.

Dave W., of Dayton, Ohio, was once a high-school hero. He ran the mile in 4:38 and was the leading hitter on his school's baseball team. But, for two decades, Dave let himself go physically. At 5'9" he weighed just about two hundred pounds. He was a bus driver. Today, his life is considerably different.

"I couldn't really say that I was bad off," he says. "I just lacked interest and excitement. I lost the spark. But I did have my family and a steady income. Of course, then, there was no way I could ever conceive of getting out and actually running. Hell, I made fun of the joggers all the time. I never wanted anyone seeing *me* out there doing that."

But then something happened that quickly changed Dave's thinking.

"I'd been feeling some pains in my chest on and off so I went to the doctor and he told me clear out of the blue that I had a dangerous heart condition. That changed everything. Of course I had to start everything gradually, but he completely changed my diet and had me doing some bicycling and pretty soon I was out there jogging."

Three things happened that surprised him: he became steadily more capable, he lost a substantial amount of weight, and he began to enjoy running.

"At first, I figured the program was going to be unbearable. I figured I'd cheat a little here and there. But after the first couple of weeks, when I could see the improvement, I had no desire whatsoever to go back to the way I was. I'd been living this kind of Archie Bunker life-style, closing my mind to a lot of things, and suddenly I saw how refreshing a jog in the park could be. Suddenly I became fitter and more vital and I really surprised myself. I mean, I really liked what was happening."

As his body changed—within eight months he was below 175—so too did his attitude.

"I'd sort of settled down, like most people do, deciding I'd gone as far as I was going to in many respects. But seeing my physical improvement made me think about what else I could do."

One thing he did was begin considering another job. He had been driving a bus for nearly a decade.

"Driving the bus was just something I felt comfortable with, it wasn't any great enjoyment. I liked it, met a lot of interesting people, but I started thinking I could do more."

Last year he quit and bought into a lucrative restaurant. But now he's even thinking beyond that. He and his wife are considering buying a motel. In the meantime, he's attending night school, taking business courses.

"I'm not sure what I'll be getting into next," forty-five-year-old Dave says, "but it'll be something new. No one can say life is over when you reach your forties. I see all sorts of new things I might get into—might even decide to go back and get a college degree.

"Let's face it, opportunities *do* tend to close up for most people as early as their late twenties. They settle down, have a family and a career. A lot of people just get fat, sit back and watch the television. They aren't challenged. I know what it's like. I decided not to be that way anymore."

Today, Dave averages forty miles a week and is even training for his first marathon, though he says, "I'm in no hurry." His weight, a year and a half later, is almost down to 160. He's long since quit smoking and considers himself a positive thinker again, something he says he stopped being before he turned thirty.

"I'll admit a couple of times over the past ten years I thought about what it'd be like if I lost weight, got in shape again. But it just never seemed realistic. Two reasons: I had this image of me getting in shape again and fitting into my old baseball uniform, but that was also a fantasy of getting young again, which wasn't possible. Reason number two: I figured that even if I did get in shape, it wouldn't make an ounce of difference mentally. I'd still be the same old guy watching the television, driving a bus. I thought this way until I was forced to change my mind. I found out I was wrong. I'd still be thinking it today if it wasn't for the doctor."

Most of our potential for success or happiness isn't realized simply because we don't act; we waste far too much time grimly repeating what we've already done before. Slaves to habit and viewpoint, we stay away from the spark that will change us.

CHAPTER FIVE

RUNNING AND STRESS

WHEN RUNNING IS APPROACHED IMPROPERLY, IT OFTEN becomes a source of stress. With Total Running, the opposite effect takes place—the stress of one's life is eased.

The correlation between running and stress was amply revealed through the survey: 79 percent said they ran, in part at least, to relieve stress. The popularity and, more essentially, the relevance of running today is perhaps best demonstrated through a discussion of stress. Modern American society, after all, is probably the most overstressed society in history. Our daily stress is responsible for the unprecedented rates of alcohol and drug abuse, suicide, and depression.

As stress authority Dr. Hans Selye, author of *The Stress of Life*, observes, the great danger of overstress is that the reserves from which we can draw to deal with stress are finite; once we have drained them, we die.

Besides my survey, evidence that exercise can relieve stress was provided by a recent survey of more than four hundred California physicians conducted by Stanford's Dr.

O. E. Byrd. The survey determined that a majority of physicians recommended exercise for their patients as a means of relieving stress.

A typical runner's explanation of the relationship between running and stress was this one provided by Tallahassee, Florida, runner Kevin B.: "I often felt tense, but I'd say I'm seldom tense anymore. That's what running has done for me."

The effect of running on stress differs with each individual, as does reaction to stress itself. Each person has his own limits, beyond which additional running will do no good. For example, just because four miles a day relaxes a person and lowers stress, there is no guarantee that six miles will relieve stress even more. Running can be an effective weapon against overstress, but it can also be misused, and when this happens, can cause additional stress.

THE STRESS OF DAILY LIFE

Dr. Hans Selye of Canada, the world's foremost authority on the subject, believes all disease is a result of too much stress. We meet stress constantly, every day, in practically everything we do. Stress occurs each time we worry about paying a bill, every time we cross a busy street or read a letter with unpleasant news.

Some of this stress is clearly necessary to our existence, but contemporary society is far too stressful. We live in an inner-directed era, sometimes interpreted as the age of narcissism. And, while some of this inner direction may be helping us solve personal difficulties, there is also an overabundance of quiet tension in need of an outlet. The approach of Total Running can serve as a much-needed outlet. In fact, many who derive mental benefits from running say they do so because they are able to use it as a release.

The most popular relievers of stress today are drugs and alcohol. Alcohol use is presently at an all-time high: 71 percent of adult Americans drink regularly, according to a Gallup poll. Dependence on prescribed tranquilizers, meanwhile, rose between 1962 and 1972 by 290 percent. Although these may be effective in temporarily relieving stress, they frequently lead to problematic consequences. Running has no such negative consequences if approached properly; this is its great advantage in combating stress.

Stress is a disease—epidemic, subtle, and often very destructive. It may create psychosomatic ailments, as well as the diseases caused by specifically physical factors. A 1978 Menninger report suggested that 70 percent of all minor ailments today are psychosomatic.

According to Dr. Barbara Brown, a researcher from UCLA Medical School, most diseases are the result of mental rather than physical dysfunction, and of a failure to determine different types of stress.

When overstressed, some people strike out, injure others, or commit crimes; others put on weight, age prematurely, lose hair, go crazy, or kill themselves. This is the "fight or flight" response. More commonly, we repress the stress, let it build, kill ourselves slowly from the inside; many commit slow suicide this way.

Dr. Brown said, "Already, what we have learned about the mind's capacity to manipulate both the body and itself—to initiate a neural process, feed back on it and change it en route—indicates that sickness need not be an inevitable part of human life."

By not realizing that our lives are too stressful, or that there are ways out of that stress, we remain susceptible to mental and physical self-destruction. By attempting to relieve stress through running, and by becoming more relaxed, we can suddenly, almost miraculously, improve and prolong our physical and mental lives, our well-being.

STRESS CONSCIOUSNESS

If the body is made better, generally the mind will be too, and emotional stress will be relieved. Lack of top physical conditioning may itself be a considerable and constant source of stress, which running can act to remove.

Gary M., from Tucson, Arizona, described the process through which his own stress was lessened through running: "I could almost literally feel the knotted muscles in my stomach: I was a bundle of nerves. I was driving myself hard, and was proud of that, but I wasn't getting any full satisfaction out of it. I tended to lose track of time; I suppose it's like a horse wearing blinders. Well, last December, a couple of guys at the plant where I work talked me into going out jogging with them one day at lunch. That first day I pretty much hated it, in fact I thought it was one of the worst things I'd ever done in my life. But I went out again a week later and it was better and then pretty soon I was doing it every day. I don't consider running the main thing in my life, but it is a great part of it; it gives a great break to my days and, you know, those knots in my stomach are gone."

RUNNING AND STRESS

We make lists of the nation's top killers—heart disease, stroke, cancer, lung disease, accidents—and isolate causes —smoking, poor diet, food additives, industrial pollution, carelessness—but we ignore what is often at the root of these problems: stress.

Why has there been such ignorance of the problems caused by stress? Dr. Selye says it is the result of a vague definition of stress. "Of course the concept of stress *is* an abstraction," he wrote, "but so is the idea of life, which could hardly be rejected as a worthless concept in biology."

Although more than three-fourths of those responding to the survey ran to relieve stress, most didn't start running for that specific reason, but found, through running, how overly stressful their lives were. A Waldorf, Maryland, runner said, "I never even realized how tense I was until I started jogging."

THE NATURE OF STRESS

There are few people who couldn't benefit by being better educated about stress. Reaction to stress varies greatly; even in identical stress situations everyone acts differently. Part of determining if your life is too stressful is studying how you handle routine stresses—crossing a street, figuring bills, etc. Are you frequently angered by minor setbacks and easily frustrated? If so, your reaction to stress may be dangerous.

Walt Schafer of the California State University sociology department said, "Two people can have virtually the same difficult experiences, yet react quite differently—one might show no symptoms of distress at all, another might become seriously ill or depressed."

Similarly, there are people who become relaxed through running more automatically than others. Why do the reactions differ and why is this important to understand? Let's look at the nature of stress.

Stress, as defined by Hans Selye, is "the state manifested by the specific syndrome which consists of all the non-specifically induced changes within a biologic system." More simply: "it suffices to keep in mind that by *stress* the physician means the common results of exposure to anything . . . . the bodily changes produced, whether a person is exposed to nervous tension, physical injury, infection, cold, heat, X rays or anything else, are what we call stress."

You will be exposed to some stress in the next five minutes. But, as was earlier described, much stress is useful. Selye, in fact, said, "Complete freedom from stress is death."

The stress process has two parts: the *stressor* and the *stress reaction*. Stressors are of three types: environmental, physiological, or psychological. An environmental stressor might be a change in temperature, eating habits, noise, work schedule; physiological stressors could be a lack of exercise (here is where running is most important), illness, physical discomfort; psychological stressors are rooted in emotions—fear, anxiety, uncertainty.

Reactions to any of these stressors vary enormously. The basic reactions are constriction of blood capillaries and a rise in blood pressure and pulse rate, along with possible cerebral congestion. Most people aren't particularly aware of either the stressors they encounter or the stress reactions that are caused. Using running to relieve stress is certainly easier if you understand stress and are aware of stressful situations. Many runners in the survey said they ran when they felt under a great deal of pressure and that they came back refreshed.

Psychological reaction to stress, which is built in and relatively easy to alter, differs dramatically among individuals. Unfortunately, the most frequent psychological means of reacting to stress is through a simple regression, becoming more withdrawn and immature, in both attitude and function. This is at best a temporary solution, which often causes a more damaging long-term stress. The great danger of stress is that our resources to combat it may be limited; if we use them up too soon we will die early.

Another danger of stress that we seldom realize is that, whether the stress is actual or imagined, the reaction will be the same. Just worrying about having an argument, for instance, will cause a stress similar to actually having that argument. The worry alone will cause adrenaline to be secreted, heart rate to rise, blood-sugar rate to increase. The body will return to relative normalcy (relative to the damage done) if the stress is removed; if it isn't removed, the system will break down, slowly at first, but eventually completely.

Psychological or emotional stress is especially damaging because it is subtler and more difficult to control than physiological or physical stress, although it too restricts blood flow and causes muscle tension, especially in the stomach and intestines. Ulcers or hypertension may result. Following either type of stress, a period of recovery is very important.

Because emotional stress is often misunderstood, recovery is more difficult to plan than recovery from a purely physical stress. Emotionally, we often unwittingly, though systematically, compound stressful reactions; we put off doing a small bit of work, then begin to worry about having to do it, sometimes giving it unrealistic or grandiose negative proportions. Stressful complications such as this can develop over something as simple as having to vacuum the living room.

The introspective aspect of running and one of the principles of Total Running is that it makes you better understand the process of your actions; it helps you see and better understand how you get into stressful situations. This is explored in the next two chapters.

THE RUNNING PERSPECTIVE

Unfortunately, most of us at one time or another persist in work or life-styles that we aren't suited for, struggling, using up the reserve of our stress reactions, burning ourselves up. We need new perspectives to see this.

Running has been referred to as a "time-out activity," which allows this much-needed perspective to determine whether our life-style is suitable. Dr. William Morgan, who has studied extensively the anxiety reactions of people who run, who meditate, and who do neither, suggests that there isn't a great deal in the running itself that makes it better than meditation; it might not be as important to run "as it is merely to take time out," he says. Taking time out from one's schedule can make one aware, through relaxation, of the overstressfulness of one's life.

Steve C., a runner from Bethesda, Maryland, described

his own reaction: "I guess the main thing running did for me was allow me to see how I was burning myself out all the time and to see that I didn't have to. I learned to relax. An evening run is one of the most relaxing things I know."

This corresponds with another result from the survey. Fifty-four percent preferred evening running as opposed to running in the morning or in the afternoon. "There's a real, almost eternal peacefulness I get from running on a cool evening," said one respondent.

Once the runner learns to use running to manage his stress he can move toward self-fulfillment. We have this one important choice: to manage stress or to let it eat away at us.

As sociology professor Walt Schafer said, "Each time we respond to a demand, large or small, our minds and bodies strive toward a new balance. . . . If these forces are handled properly, they can contribute to a more complete realization of our potentialities—one psychologist has referred to this as self-actualization."

Use running when your life seems too stressful.

MANAGING STRESS

There is no magical scale which tells a runner that his level of stress requires that he run 3⅜ miles per day and another runner that he run 4½ miles. The individual nature of stress prevents this. The most essential step to managing stress is trying to become more relaxed. But when relaxation has been learned, running should then be used so that the runner may become more aware of the process of stress.

Relaxation will create a sanctuary and a new perspective.

The runner should use this development. His relaxed state will isolate him, partially at least, from the stressors in his life and will give him the chance to notice stressful situations as they approach. Once a person is able to recognize stressors, he can go through the process of self-education by seeing which situations in his life are most stressful; then he can consciously avoid them, whenever possible.

An example of this is Patricia S., a high-school English teacher from Montana, who said, "Being wrapped up in myself is something I know a lot about. I was just looking at the ground all the time, imagining how great my problems were and trying to figure them out twenty-four hours a day, even in sleep. I could see problems coming a mile away and I'd always think, 'I won't let that happen again,' but before I knew it, there it was again, and I was figuring out ways out of the same old situations.

"After I began running, I decided not to ever think about anything negative during the time I was on a run, and it's really worked wonders. I began to see problems approaching me and I'd think, 'I don't have to let them get me down, I can be carefree like I am while running.' And it's worked."

The most harmful stresses in our lives can be removed through this simple process of stepping back, relaxing, and watching them as they approach.

Running philosopher George Sheehan recently said, "My task is to know myself, to see with my own eyes, to recognize my good and evil, to learn whether I am primarily made for fight or flight, to understand what stresses I handle best. I must know what strengthens me and what could destroy me, how to impose stress that makes me better, how to minimize or avoid that which is hostile to me."

Clearly, running is the type of stress that makes us better, and that also minimizes negative stress. But it's a process that involves self-examination. If there is no self-examination, no deliberate thought about our own individual stresses, the running itself can become an additional stress. This is why no absolutes, no definitive schedules are being proposed here.

How much running? Try what you can handle; evaluate what it does to the stress in your life. The average number of miles per week in the survey was 29, with one runner claiming an average of 105 and another just 5 miles.

FREEDOM

Although diseases with specific causes have decreased, degenerative and stress-related diseases have steadily increased. This is because we carry the cage of our stress with us at all times and, despite what some think, money and status have no power to remove it. As Hans Selye said, "The more man learns about ways to combat external causes of death (germs, cold, hunger), the more likely is he to die from his own voluntary suicidal actions."

Many of our habits are unknowingly suicidal; every day we take a step closer to killing ourselves. It's not something, though, that we think about or often consider. Because it is drug-like, stress becomes addictive. We metamorphose, in this way, into beings who are comfortable, though not content, with great self-destructive stresses. It is often a fear of withdrawal that keeps us this way. For many, running becomes a self-treatment for their addiction. It reduces the need for great stress by creating positive, more relaxed habits.

Selye mentioned this possible connection, based on one's approach to exercise, in *The Stress of Life*: "We say that our muscles limber up during exercise and that we are thrilled by great emotional experiences; all this prepares us for better peak accomplishments. On the other hand, there is the tingling sensation, the jitteriness, when we are too keyed up. This impairs our work."

We have the choice to pursue a less stressful life-style, or to remain addicted to stress. As we cease to become victims of stress, we become more free as well.

CHAPTER SIX

RUNNING AND MEDITATION

AFTER RUNNING HAS BECOME A POSITIVE INFLUENCE ON your life-style, there is a deeper level of insight that can be cultivated, leading to profound states of relaxation, Zen-like awakening, and spiritual and astral experiences. It all begins with meditation.

With the proper use of concentration and meditation exercises, running can become a form of meditation that might make your life fuller and more relaxed. You will learn to avoid distracting thoughts and nagging worries, and you will move even farther from the overstressed life-style discussed in the previous chapter.

Meditation can be defined as exercise in contemplation. There is always some contemplation on a run, but the goal now is to deepen it. This will lead to the mental states of Zen and spiritualism discussed in the next few chapters, which can erase certain problems and may make you feel continually young.

Exercise plays a role in all meditation. Even the most

101

formal meditations stress the importance of exercising, of keeping the muscles loose and relaxed. In fact, some formal meditations, such as Chinese Zen, have discarded the idea of the sitting "lotus" position. Rather, they prefer "walking meditation," and take long walks between mountain temples.

With the proper practice, running can become informal meditation, a transference into another activity of the state of mind reached in formal meditation. In fact, many of the same exercises used in formal meditation can be used in running.

Ed M., a Los Angeles runner, priest, and meditator, said of the relationship between running and meditation: "The spiritual effects of running are the same as those experienced in meditation. At first, for a beginner, meditation is different from anything else. For the beginning runner, running is different from everything else. But both become the same after a while."

In meditation, the goal is to reach a unique state of mind in which you are completely inner directed. The intention is to recognize yourself as a pure entity, an idea. Meditators who practice in the lotus position say their goal is to become and think as a triangle, with their knees and buttocks forming the base. For the period of time in which they can maintain this state, they say they are able to block out pain and worries. They are pure entity, a triangle, not a complex human being with complex human problems.

In running, the athlete strives to become an efficient, effortless running machine. He tries, in other words, not to be aware of the physical act of his running.

This is what Joe Henderson described as "meditation on

the move." It is something that requires discipline and practice.

The purpose of meditation, the reason you should want to make your running meditative, is subtle and all-encompassing: so that you can have a clearer vision, more self-assurance, and better understanding of your own psyche.

As Christmas Humphreys wrote in his book, *Concentration and Meditation*: "[the purpose] is threefold: to dominate the lower, separative self, to develop the mind's own higher faculties toward a vision of life's essential unity, and to unite this dual process in one continuous spiritual unfolding."

BEGINNING

Creating a state of meditation while running is very similar to creating one in formal meditation. The exercises explained in this chapter are all also applicable to sitting meditation.

The counting method introduced in Chapter Two is the best way to start, but if you have trouble doing it, try another of the following exercises. Or, alternate those exercises with the counting exercise. This is how it's done:

Begin by breathing in just through your nostrils, letting the air come in naturally; don't suck it in. Exhale completely, making sure all the air has left your lungs before you inhale again. As you exhale, count "one." Repeat this. As you exhale again, count "two." Once you've counted to ten, go back to one. Try this for a period of about five minutes on a run and build to fifteen minutes or more.

The point of the exercise is to develop the concentration

necessary for deeper forms of meditative relaxation. The counting is a first step in this development. You should be striving to clear your mind of all thoughts as you do the counting. At first, this may seem tedious, and you might become restless. But as you practice, it will eventually become easier and more enjoyable.

All beginning meditation exercises are primarily intended to develop concentration; they are largely disciplinary, though there can be some insight and illumination as they transpire. Counting is just one beginning exercise. Here are some others:

Object Meditation. This is one of the traditional beginning meditative exercises, done from a sitting position. It involves sitting and staring at an object—traditionally a candle flame. A runner isn't going to be able to concentrate on a small stationary object such as a candle flame for very long unless he runs in a circle. But runners report object meditation nevertheless: they meditate on the ocean, on mountains, even on cracks in the sidewalk.

A runner from Thurmont, Maryland, said, "Sometimes when I'm running I'll sort of hypnotize myself. There's this big hill I always run near and I just stare at it for a real long time and eventually if I do it long enough, I forget I'm running. The hill becomes a magnet, pulling me toward it."

This is the process of object meditation. Use a hill, a tall building, a lake, anything that is stationary and prominent. Start by looking at the object and thinking about it— its physical properties, how it came to be, how old it is, etc. Then, move your thoughts away from the nature of the object. Clear your mind of thought and just stare at and concentrate on the object itself. As with counting, practice this each run, beginning with five to ten minutes and steadily increasing. The difficulty with this exercise is that when you are staring at the object, it will be difficult to keep your thoughts from drifting. This is where disciplined practice and concentration are essential.

When developed, this exercise can produce insights. Runners frequently describe various degrees of altered perception if they continually stare at a single object while running. And this will also lead you on to the higher forms of meditation.

Thought Watching. This is the ideal beginning exercise, since it is at the base of all meditation exercises. But it will take practice before you can do it effectively. The idea is to become so relaxed that you seem to separate from your stream of consciousness: you view your thoughts as they pass through your mind. Study them, ask yourself why they occur, observe how one thought leads to another, how each one connects. Try this for several-minute intervals as you run. This is where the beginner's experience with meditation can be most profound, first because thought watching is a learning process and second because knowledge of the origins of your thoughts is the most effective way to become relaxed and free from the bonds of habit.

Visualization. Another common meditation exercise is visualizing, imagining an object to exist or imagining yourself to be in a different location. This is creative meditation, and is best practiced only after the earlier, more disciplinary forms have been learned. The basis of this was explained in the relaxation chapter.

The simplest type of visualization is to mentally recreate an object you have just looked at. In formal meditation this is done by staring briefly at an object, closing your eyes, and then attempting to recreate that object in your mind. You can do this while running without closing your eyes. For instance, look at a car, turn your head, and visualize the car in a neighbor's front yard. Try doing this for as long as you can.

More interesting is to imagine an object to exist or another person to be running with you, and to use your imagination to make that person more real. "Run" with an old friend you haven't seen in years. A variation of this is *transport visualization*, in which you imagine yourself in different surroundings; this can be another part of town or another part of the world.

Try these exercises, or improvise your own. The essential goals are these: work first on developing a disciplined concentration, then on a greater insight into your own thinking process.

Joe Henderson has these three simple rules for cultivating meditative running: run without an end in sight, always run a little even if it feels bad at first, and let the pace find itself.

Practice clearing your mind of all thought; this ability is at the core of the running meditation experience, and can be profound at other times in your life. For instance, when you can't get to sleep at night, the immediate reason is that you can't stop a certain flow of thoughts in your mind that isn't conducive to sleep. Similarly, whenever you can't concentrate on work, the reason is that the thoughts in your mind aren't conducive to what you're working on. When you meditate, you develop your imagination without sacrificing your ability to concentrate, and you learn to clear your mind.

To develop this state, begin by following the exercises as written, but gradually follow your intuition and improvise to find variations that are most personally effective.

Strive to develop a little bit on each run. If one exercise isn't working, try another. Try to develop an understanding of the process of your thinking. That is most essential.

As Joseph Goldstein, author of several books on meditation, said, "[Active meditation] is not really an exercise in movement. It is an exercise in mindfulness. Use the movement to develop a careful awareness. . . . Experiment. The essential thing is to be mindful, to be aware of what's happening."

Use the basic exercises until they become too routine—probably after several weeks—then you can move on to the higher states of meditation and the practice of meditating on a phrase.

PASSING THE BARRIER

As anyone interested in it will soon find out, meditation isn't a retreat. It's a difficult exercise in self-discipline, which demands a great deal of willpower. At first, the exercises may seem tedious, trying, uninteresting. They may even seem to contradict the whole philosophy of running as pleasure. But occasionally they will be enlightening, particularly when they involve an exploration of your thinking process. And they will make you better able to relax.

The discipline of meditation will evolve into a state of

greater self-understanding. We gain new perspectives after we have passed the initial stage of discipline. The most difficult task will be keeping away distractions. At first, the meditation state will be nothing but a condition of distractions. This can make the entire process seem unpleasant; it is the hardest part. Once it is mastered, though, the rewards are available.

The initial discipline is what teaches us about distractions in our thinking. We pick up our most distracting habits unconsciously, and usually aren't aware of the extent they affect us or even that we have them . . . certainly not that we are dependent on them. Meditation, in its earliest steps, forces us to see the effects of these habits. At first this may be almost unbearable. But if we can admit the existence of these distractions, meditation can remove them, not only in the daily moments of meditation, but in all moments of our lives, even when we are not meditating.

Eventually, the discomfort will pass as the mind is able to become free of the distractions; then the running itself will change too. It will become gentler, more regularly appreciated. It might be less randomly profound, but it will be more uniform and valuable.

According to Ed M., "The so-called high is merely a mind that is clear, functioning at one hundred percent. Most beginning runners and Zen students achieve this state only rarely. But by and by, this state becomes more and more common, until it is the usual state of mind, it is no longer recognizable as a special state. Thus, experienced runners and Zen priests, monks, etc. rarely talk of 'spiritual highs' because they are high all of the time. But this high is their ordinary state."

RUNNING AND MEDITATION

Ed believes that the best method of reaching the desired state of, as he puts it, "attaining a total mind all of the time" is to practice a regular program of running and meditation.

MEDITATION ON A PHRASE

Once the beginning exercises have been learned and developed, the runner should practice meditating on a phrase. This is similar to the counting exercise, only instead of a number, a phrase or a question is used. In formal meditation, these phrases are called *koans*.

The *koan* is an anecdote created by the Zen masters. Practically, though, the runner can use any question or idea of a thought-provoking nature. It can be a line from a popular song, something you read in a newspaper. The Zen requirement for a *koan* is simply that it deal with some aspect of Truth.

Proceed just as you did with the counting. Think out the phrase each time you exhale. Don't consciously analyze it, just say it in your mind, let it pass through your mind, let your subconscious think about it. Learn to block out extraneous thoughts from interfering with the repeating of this phrase.

The effect of meditating on the *koan* will initially be less uniform than in the counting stage, but where the latter might have become drab and uninteresting, this form of meditation will push you into new depths of relaxation and might even lead to euphoric experience. At first, it will create a new tension as the runner strives for a deeper concentration, but this tension will pass. Alternate the

109

phrases you use in this exercise, as some will be more effective than others. When one seems especially effective, practice it several days in succession. If one is difficult and unpleasant, don't persist with it too long.

The point of the *koan*, Suzuki said, is "to awaken the student's mind to the fact that what he has so far accepted as commonplace fact or as a logical impossibility, is not necessarily so, and that his former way of looking at things was not always correct or helpful to his spiritual welfare. . . . To force the student to assume this inquiring attitude is the aim of the *koan*."

It is an exercise in discipline, too. There will be the temptation to stop repeating the phrase; this must be resisted. There will be the temptation to think of other thoughts. But as this too is resisted, you will be able to reach toward greater self-understanding.

AUTOMATIC WRITING

The greatest benefits of running are possible only if you can break through the strict barriers of your thinking. This book is intended to help you do just that. As each exercise works you will learn more about yourself; the exercises may elucidate hopes and repressed personality conflicts. The goal is to get steadily closer to your essence. As the barriers are broken, you surprise yourself as you learn who you are and at the same time you surprise yourself with the potential you have. Total Running involves a rooting into the subconscious mind, breaking through the barriers of conscious thinking.

An exercise with a similar profound effect is automatic writing. This can be used along with the meditation practice. Automatic writing is sitting down and for a period of time—fifteen minutes is a good start, though it should build to thirty minutes or more—writing the first thoughts that come into your mind, not taking the time to think out thoughts, but writing down images as they pass through your mind. Many people who do this for a while find themselves remembering scenes and people· that they had long since pressed out of their conscious memory. After you have done this free-form exercise, examine what you have written. If some things you wrote puzzle you, think about them, particularly in connection with the images before and after them. This is similar to watching the process of your thoughts, but it is easier to study, because the writing acts as a freezing of thoughts.

The principle of this type of writing is similar to that of the inner-directed running: you can do either activity on a conscious, predictable level or you can give it greater meaning, breaking through the barriers of your conscious thinking and turning it into a self-educating, subconscious activity. Because the initial problem of breaking into the subconscious is the same, one type of subconscious training, such as automatic writing, will aid another, such as running.

With practice, we can unearth the repressed parts of our minds, and in so doing try to solve the problems of our personality that our normal conscious thinking ignores.

"Automatic writing in the simplest form," wrote Anita M. Muhl, M.D., in her book, *Automatic Writing, An Approach to the Unconscious,* may be defined as script which . . . [is produced] *involuntarily* and in some instances without his [the writer's] being aware of the process, although he may be (and generally is) in an alert waking state . . . . everything we sense (hear, see, feel, taste, touch) whether we are aware of it or not, is recorded and can be recalled under proper conditions, perhaps a fair idea of just how complicated we really are. . . . Even those who have been psychoanalyzed and are fairly well acquainted with their own thought processes, their conflicts and their limitations, are constantly being tripped up by their estimates of themselves and in their interpretation of their own actions.

Inner-directed running requires and develops an understanding of your motives and essence. This may be difficult at first, but with concentration the barriers of your formal thinking can be broken through. Automatic writing, like meditation, is one means of doing this.

THE INNER CONTROL OF EXTERIORS

Meditation is a first step in understanding why you think as you do, in understanding that you are largely what you are because of your thought process. Your thoughts determine what you do. Often a thought is planted in your subconscious and you are hardly aware of it, even as it grows into your consciousness. Sometimes these thoughts can be negative and harmful.

An example was given by a runner from East Lansing, Michigan, who said of her habits, "There was a pattern of mild self-destructiveness and it had a lot to do with seeing

other people. I'd see people on TV who would get drunk
every day and I thought that was something that people
did. It was more of a subconscious thing, where I just ad-
mired that kind of way of life in a very subliminal manner
and it was my rationalization. When I started running, it
did things for me, for real, and I found that the most content people don't get drunk every afternoon."

With your thoughts you can change your appearance and
your behavior. You first plant the idea and then carry it
out. Meditation is an initial step in digging into your subconscious to unearth the seeds of inaction that have been
planted by negative thoughts. Combined with the positive
healthy aspect of running, meditation is an ideal means of
coming to terms with the negativity of your thoughts. With
meditation and running, you become aware of your thinking and try to understand and control the intricate relationship between your body and your mind. You realize in a
positive manner how your mind controls your body and
how, by giving attention to your mind, to your thinking,
you can change your body.

Jane Roberts explained this relationship in the book,
The Nature of Personal Reality:

> . . . you can become healthy if you are ill, slim if you are
> overweight, gain weight if you prefer or alter your physical
> image in profound fashion through the use of your ideas and
> beliefs.
>
> They form the blueprint by which you make your body,
> whether you have known this or not. Your body is an artistic
> creation, formed and constantly maintained at unconscious
> levels, but quite in line with your beliefs about what and who
> you are.

RIGID THINKING

Try this when you run: tell yourself you have forgotten all you know; tell yourself you are a child; tell yourself you know nothing and want to learn, but you only want to learn what you can find out for yourself, not what other people can tell you. Assume all you have known previously is false. Take individual notions you have and tear them down. For instance, if you have cynical ideas about religion, ask yourself why you have them. Think about how they come to be. Try to remove the notions. This is the process that is necessary for you to begin probing into your deeper motivations and ideas.

Tom P. is a Detroit runner who spent two years in a seminary, has studied meditation and Zen, and currently works as an editor of religious texts. He described how he clears his mind of rigid thinking while running: "I try not to take on ideas that are not based on sound reasoning. I try not to become swayed by passion. But I think all humans are susceptible to adopting notions and attitudes automatically, for reasons they don't understand. I've found that you can use the run to break yourself away from these. It's similar to meditation. I begin by thinking about what wrong I have ever done. By this I mean what actions I have taken that I've later regretted. I examine these and think about my attitude at the time and ask myself why I took that action if I was going to regret it later. What in my personality led me to that? For example, if I told a sincere, honest friend I was busy just because I didn't want to see him, I ask myself why and I find out that I have a tendency to be insecure around that person. Then I probe deeper. I ask why I tend to be insecure, and I discover that I am afraid of that person's conception of me. I am afraid to be myself near that person because he thinks I'm very strait-laced. I'm afraid to drink a beer around that person. I then tell myself I shouldn't be running from that person. I should admit who I am to that person. So once I've decided this, I run and I feel good because I have just solved a problem of my being. I try to do this often."

This self-discovery is an individual process that you have to be alone to experience. It breaks through all intellectual barriers. It is a truth, beyond rationalization, that we are seeking. It will bring a positive feeling that intellectual thinking will never produce.

"Those to whom a sense of the individuality of all apparently divided things is alive and a wonderful reality need no intellectual argument to support their knowledge of the Self's essential unity," wrote Christmas Humphreys in his book *Concentration and Meditation*. "Though their feet be still of clay, their eyes have seen the light reflected from Enlightenment, and though the vision be above description save in a richly coloured symbolism common to them all, yet they *know* as a spiritual experience truths which can never be understood with the cumbrous mechanism of the intellectual mind. This does not mean that the mystic can avoid the warfare of the selves, but that his method of dealing with the problem is fundamentally different.

Meditation, and meditative running, begin this process.

CHAPTER SEVEN

RUNNING AND ZEN

FROM MEDITATION, THE INTEGRATION OF ZEN IDEAS IS the next step in the development of running as a positive total activity.

Zen literally means meditation, but the implications go beyond meditation. It is also a philosophy and a way of life, particularly relevant in our contemporary society. The Zen way of life—self-enlightenment, contemplation without procrastination—has had a great effect on the nature of current thinking. Although many of its principles and most of its terminology haven't been accepted by great numbers of people, several of the basic ideas have.

The goal of inner-directed Total Running is to make the runner Zen-like—more enlightened, content, and free. As Japanese Zen master Suzuki wrote, "Zen in its essence is the art of seeing into the nature of one's own being and it points the way from bondage to freedom."

The Zen philosophy meshes very well with running. The timelessness, the introspective and intense personal sensations that runners talk about, are very Zen-like. Valerie

TOTAL RUNNING

Andrews wrote, in *The Psychic Power of Running*:

> In running, as in Zen, we face a wedge of boredom, a chunk
> of empty time that separates our usual compulsive thinking
> from a state of altered awareness. In this interface, we sim-
> ply watch the movement of our thoughts across the prosce-
> nium of consciousness, without exerting judgment or choice;
> at the same time, we allow the body to find a rhythm of its
> own, and let the action of the run be formed from within.
> Preoccupation with goals often interferes with our ability to
> let the body flow, to experience "empty time."

As with religion, there are various forms of Zen, each of
which claims to be the true one. For instance, Zen Buddhism advocates thinking of good, whereas Zazen (Japanese Zen) says, "Neither think of good nor evil" and also
"forsake the world and Buddhism."

For every runner there is an individual best application
of Zen to running.

THINKING AND ACTION

In Zen you attempt to encompass in one activity the total
meaning of your existence. A Zen practitioner can be content washing windows all his life, if he gives that action the
proper depth of meaning. That is what we are doing in running. As one writer recently said, in the process of a single
run you struggle, you create, you love, you are happy and
sad, you experience nature with all of your senses.

You can either take all of this for granted, as many do,
or you can learn to experience those feelings; and then
running, like anything else, can have a profound personal
significance.

The example is given in Zen literature of a man who is about to dive from a tall rock into the sea; the man will stand there, even after deciding he wants to do it, and wonder about the distance of the jump, worry about the water, think about the impact. This is how most people act. Before experiencing something, they first contemplate it, imagine what it will feel like. And by so doing, they create expectations that blur the actual experience.

The Zen way is not to contemplate but to actually *do it*, to experience the event rather than contemplate what the event will be like. Running should become like that. You shouldn't worry for hours beforehand what course you are going to run, how far or how fast. You should just be eager to run, and decide the specifics once you get out there. The problem with forcing yourself through a preplanned run that isn't fulfilling is that the next day you'll remember the unpleasantness and will be less eager and more contemplative about your running. You may begin to wonder each day if you really want to do it. The Zen approach to doing anything is to carry out the act in full, clear awareness, rather than to deliberate and create expectations and unnecessary worry and fear.

THE GLOW

In true Zen experiences you find great significance in simple, usually overlooked places. You might start laughing uncontrollably at the way a piece of paper is blown across a street; you may feel deep sympathy for a small child who is pressing a button to cross a busy intersection, you may have an intense feeling of freedom watching a bird spread its wings. You suddenly let your emotions free and they experience the world without intellectual blinders. It's a unique and intense experience, yet quite simple.

Sometimes this untapping of the emotions seems to create a glowing sensation. The world—trees, flowers, bushes, mountains, people—seems to emit a glow; through that glow you suddenly know the essence of things and people, an essence you would normally never consider.

So-called peak running experiences have this Zen-like intensity. My own intense run, which happened on Hallowe'en night 1975, illustrates this. It began with a release unrelated to running. I had just written several personally satisfying stories and they had gone over well in the writing class I was taking. The success of the stories seemed to free my subconscious; it was a personal breakthrough. I had a very positive-charged, somewhat giddy state of mind. It was twilight when I walked back from that writing class to get ready for my run. As I started out, I seemed to sense a glow around the buildings near where I lived. It was something my imagination had created many times before; usually it quickly disappeared as I turned my thinking inward.

But on this occasion, I embraced this glowing sensibility and the run was uniquely smooth and euphoric for its entire thirty minutes. I had never had a run like this one. This time everything was special. There seemed to be a spiritual significance to the smiles of pumpkins on front porches; the darkening sky, with its shades of gray and black and faded orange, meshed into an eerie abstract painting.

Dark barren cornfields symbolized change; traffic lights

signified the order man has had to instill in society; car lights switching on symbolized how our sophisticated society is at the mercy of the simple unchangeable laws of nature; a football team practicing signified man's need to play and his desire to excel; the sound of my own footsteps echoing in the darkness explained the importance of each man alone in this world, deriving an enjoyment from his actions even when no one can see him.

And what made the run especially extraordinary were the children going from door to door for Hallowe'en candy, dressed in costumes, carrying out their annual ritual, and feeling special about it. It was a celebration, and I seemed to feel its importance as I ran. It was a celebration I understood—a celebration of release; they were gathering and eating as much candy as they could on this one day as a release from the 364 days of the year when it was discouraged. The pumpkins I had seen for weeks on front-porch stoops seemed to be heralding this ritual! This was what they had been grown and harvested for. At the end of the night, their use over, some would be smashed in the street. There would be other mischief—toilet paper in trees and soap inscriptions on car windows. During the ritual, the celebration, these things were accepted. I suddenly understood all of this, and the effect was an awakening.

All of these thoughts passed through my mind, but not in a contemplative or reflective manner. I didn't think about any of them. They flowed. Each was a separate realization. It was as if all the meanings of our existence were suddenly becoming clear to me in the scenario of a half-hour run on Hallowe'en night. This is the Zen state of mind.

There seemed to be a positive glow about the entire run.

It wasn't planned. I haven't had a run so intense since, and I had no idea beforehand that I would have one that day either. But factors combined and it happened. Factors have to combine; it's much harder when you try to combine them yourself.

THE NATURE OF ZEN

Zen is a process, an approach to life. The philosophy behind Zen is often described by Buddhist concepts. It is based on our Three Signs of Being: impermanence, non-I (egolessness), and suffering. Suffering occurs only because we can't accept impermanence and non-I. The reason we cannot accept them is because of the Three Fires that burn in everyone: wanting, hating, and delusion.

From these ideas comes the basis of Zen—The Four Noble Truths. These are: there is suffering, physical and mental disease; there is a cause of this suffering; this cause can be worked out in our minds; this cause can be brought to an end. This is the formal basis of Zen. The practical basis of Zen is experiencing the totality of what we do, clearing the obstructive barriers to our thinking.

Zen is the simplification of one's life to hasten self-understanding. The nature of Zen and the nature and evolution of inner-directed Total Running are explained in this Zen idea: "While the walker follows the Way, the Way itself is the discipline which produces clear seeing and the strength to act in accordance with it. Then the Way ends; the walker is free of the Way, free of his own I-based biased and deluded seeing. He himself has become the Way. So he acts out of his own nature."

122

This is the goal of Zen: to be freed from our preconceptions and in so doing to elucidate our true nature, through meditation and action.

Zen is first a breaking down of the pointless cyclic nature of our action and satisfaction. The cycles of ups and downs and the pursuit of goals which, when attained, fail to produce the expected satisfactions, often occupy our attention and lead us to ignore the matter of our essence.

Zen is goalless. It is an ongoing process of inner clarification. As in meditation, where you watched your thoughts, here you watch the process of your actions and desires, and in this way gain a greater self-understanding. One of the first steps is cultivating a state of humility.

The Zen analogy is of the ocean and the waves. Waves are raised by storms of passion and become very visible. But they are still part of the ocean, their water will return to it. We are not waves, we are ocean, though we may be persuaded, deluded, by the waves.

THE ZEN SAYINGS AND QUESTIONS

There are hundreds of Zen sayings, questions, stories, and *koans* which are designed to allow a better personal understanding of Zen. Ponder these sayings as you run, meditate on them as you did on inspirational phrases in the last chapter. They should develop in your mind an understanding of the essence of Zen, but more important for this book, they are inspiring and can make your running more fulfilling.

• The wise man does nothing; the fool ties himself up.

• When hungry I eat; when tired I sleep. Fools laugh at me. The wise understand.

• Four billion people live on a ball. The ball is suspended in nothing. What are these four billion people doing on the ball? And why do you want to know?

• To reach real gentleness means to let the original nature persist in all circumstances of everyday life.

• The secret of seeing things as they are is to take off your colored spectacles.

• You can hear the sound of two hands clapping. Now show me the sound of one hand.

• If you meet a swordsman on the road, show him your sword. Do not offer your poem to a man who is not a poet.

• Rather than putting the body to rest, rest the heart.

• Without speaking, without silence, can you still express the truth? How?

• The flower petals fall though we love them, the weeds grow though we hate them.

• If you know that fundamentally there is nothing to seek, you have settled your affairs.

• The painted picture of a dumpling does not take away one's hunger.

• We all have a light inside; but trying to look at it makes it turn black.

• Hide your good deeds and keep your functioning secret. Look like a simpleton or a fool.

• If no one has put you under restraint, why then do you ask to be liberated?

• Getting rid of things and clinging to emptiness are the same illness. It is like throwing oneself into fire to avoid being drowned.

• All things come from the One, but where does the One come from?

• Though descriptions can be given, what really matters cannot be rendered in words.

• Why does the enlightened man not stand on his feet and explain himself?

THE ZEN ATTITUDE

Running will be more fulfilling with the Zen attitude. But Zen is a perspective that must be developed. The Zen attitude is the ability to transcend stubborn ideas and stoppages in your thinking. It is explained in this Chinese Zen proverb: "Where there is an impasse, there is a way out." The acceptance of barriers without any fears destroys the false appearances of those barriers. Through Zen, you overcome barriers not with strategy and force, but through transcendence. Barriers disappear, not because you find the solution to the problem, but because you perceive that in reality there never was a problem.

The basis of running as a Zen act is to transcend the mundane difficulties of physical discomfort, anxiety, sore legs, etc. Of course, if the physical discomfort persists and seems to be more than soreness, then it is best to see a doctor. But if it is just the common discomfort that sometimes accompanies running, this can be transcended. When you reach a state of mind in which you no longer recognize the physical discomforts of running, then Zen enlightenment is possible.

"The object in Zen discipline," wrote Suzuki, "consists

in acquiring a new viewpoint for looking into the essence of things." The Zen attitude doesn't take perceptions for granted. When you run with this attitude, you appreciate the significance of cracks in the sidewalk, of chipped paint on fences.

Zen, like the running philosophy of this book, is also an attitude about goals. The Zen idea is not to seek greater plateaus, but to better understand the plateau you are on. One of the more common Zen examples that shows the importance of this attitude, as well as the futility of constantly striving for unreachable goals, is this one: Man is enslaved, trapped in a box. The Zen idea of attaining freedom is to do so without breaking the box, i.e., to become free inside the box before trying to be free outside of it. The reasoning is that if you aren't free within the box, you won't be free when you break the box, either: there will just be another, larger box.

THE ZEN LIFE-STYLE

Zen is a way of life. It is a nonaggressive, unselfish search for personal understanding and meaning. Its followers believe that if its ideas were spread, the problems of society would disappear. Zen master Roshi said, "When people know themselves and have their own strength, they do not need government. Otherwise they are just a mob and must be ruled. On the other hand, when the rulers do not know themselves, they push the people around."

Not all of the Zen philosophy is accessible. But there are a number of objectives for how a person lives his life that can give the runner a better appreciation for Zen and can hasten the progression of Total Running. These can be pondered on a run or used as objectives for life-style. They are (from Zen master Rinzai):

• Seek nothing from without. Then you are a Buddha.
• It is only because our wisdom is screened by our feelings and our substance changed by our thoughts that we endure suffering.
• Accept things as they are. Don't worry about them. Walk when you want to walk. Sit when you want to sit.
• Be simple and unconcerned in your doings, whether it's wearing clothes, eating, or making decisions.
• Doubt is a demon.

By these rules, life-style becomes more positive, much as it does when you first begin to derive the benefits of running. This is a further development of the positive feeling that came when you started running. It is a less doubtful, more active way of life.

"What is important is how we live our lives," wrote Irmgard Schloegl in *The Wisdom of Zen Masters*. "And the wonderful thing is that once this is realized, then our life has of itself taken on meaning and purpose, it has become 'full' when it seemed empty before."

Zen and Total Running are experiences of perception and feeling that drive to the roots of intelligence simply because they aren't intellectual. As Paul Weinhold wrote, "The Zen student is told to feel the force of the universe behind him. One day he does."

When this happens, you experience the enlightenment of Zen running.

TOTAL RUNNING

ZEN AND ENLIGHTENMENT

A discussion of running euphorias was presented in an earlier chapter. The Zen euphoria is different, more evolved, as it requires a devotion to Zen ideals, thinking, and discipline. Called *satori*, the Zen enlightenment represents a breakthrough in one's attitude, an idea that is spontaneous and that suddenly makes long-held intellectual ideas irrelevant. *Satori* is an intense sensation that runners can achieve if they become properly relaxed. It is the sudden understanding that past worries were silly and unnecessary; an equally sudden sense of possibility; a realization that one's personal life is a career.

Satori, wrote Alan Watts, is "the sudden realization of the truth of Zen."

Satori can be simple and still profound, because it is a fresh base, a uniquely clear perception uncluttered by cynicism and preconceptions. This is the goal of Zen. The illuminations are like fireworks, quick mental-orgasmic realizations of new viewpoint, breaking through long-held suppositions.

Each time this happens, there is an evolution; in effect it is a training procedure, in which the practitioner learns to act without being swayed by preconceptions. He gets closer to his own essence.

We learn what our intuitive nature is during these enlightenments. "The single aim of the true Zen follower is to so train his mind that all thought processes based on the dualism inseparable from 'ordinary' life are transcended, their place being taken by that Intuitive Knowledge which, for the first time, reveals to a man what he really is," wrote John Blofeld in *The Zen Teaching of Huang Po: On the Transmission of the Mind.*

ZEN DIET

Diet has an influence on running, both physically and psychologically. The wrong food may cause indigestion and make your run unpleasant; it might lead you to think that the running itself is at fault, or your attitude, rather than the diet.

Zen has a strict diet philosophy based on moderation. The philosophy is to eat to survive, not for the pleasure of taste. Overeating makes a person sluggish, less alert, and it disrupts his digestive system.

Zen master Keizan expressed this philosophy about food:

> In eating, avoid anything unripe, indigestible, rotten or unsanitary. And do not eat too much or fill up with delicacies. Such gorging will not only increase your discomfort during zazen [the Japanese form of Zen meditation] but will show everyone that you are not free from avarice. Food exists only to support life; do not cling to the taste of it.

THE DEVOTION OF ZEN

The relationship between running and Zen involves the acceptance and application of a philosophy, rather than a list of exercises that must be practiced. Zen running requires a devotion which begins to make running religious and spiritual.

Start by just thinking of the Zen philosophy as you run.

Meditate on the Zen sayings. At first, do this only as it feels comfortable, until the ideas of Zen come to take on a personal meaning. Then do it more regularly; either meditate on a Zen idea each run or think in a Zen fashion. This will make your runs calmer and more important.

"Zen makes a religion of tranquillity," wrote Sokei-An, in *The World of Zen*. "Zen is not a religion which arouses emotions, causing tears to roll down from your eyes or stirring us to shout aloud the name of God. . . . You do not come to this moment through logic or philosophy."

The devotion to Zen can enhance your devotion to running.

THE LIMITS OF ZEN

There are limits to how valuable Zen can be without it becoming detrimental to one's family, social, and business life. And there are some points of Zen that are inaccessible to the average person. Zen endows a runner with greater self-understanding and contentment; for this, the full Zen doctrine needn't be followed. Rather, use just what fits into your life-style.

Although the Zen idea of moderation is a good one, an occasional excess in running can be revitalizing and can keep away boredom. Moderation is valuable in developing the discipline of Zen and meditation, but if you feel like doing an unusually long, difficult, or slightly crazy run, that can be very beneficial as a release, assuming it is done occasionally and doesn't disrupt the mental state that has been cultivated.

In his book *Feast of Fools*, Harvey Cox talked about the

need for release, for occasional excess. He described a
medieval holiday in parts of Europe in which once a year
a wild, soul-cleansing celebration occurred, from which no
one was excused. No office or institution was excused from
ridicule. Everyone had to wear masks and mix with everyone else. It was a complete release, a breaking of long-
existing barriers of order and sensibility. Cox theorized
that a similar feast today could work wonders for modern
civilization, that it could teach us about who we are.

"It suggests that work, however rewarding, is not the
highest end of life but must contribute to personal human
fulfillment," Cox wrote.

> We need stated times for non-work to remind us that not
> even an astronomical gross national product and total em-
> ployment can bring a people salvation. . . . Festivity, like
> play, contemplation and making love, is an end in itself. It is
> not instrumental.

The main thing a runner should consider about the limits
of Zen in relation to his running is the effect a commitment
to Zen ideas might have on his personal life. Certainly
many of the basic Zen ideas are inimical to progress and
to maintaining one's place in society. The ultimate Zen
state of mind is virtually impossible to attain if you work
eight hours a day, have three kids, and own a house in
suburbia.

The Zen philosophy promotes isolation and while this,
as part of learning of yourself, is valuable, as a life commitment it would disrupt family and social affairs.

Additionally, there are some ideas in Zen that seem un-
desirable not only in the context of society, but in terms

of personal happiness. In the pursuit of moderation, some Zen masters advocate the forsaking of joy and love. Sometimes the Zen insistence on forsaking normal human emotions, even positive ones, seems cynical.

From Zen master Rinzai: "If you give rise to a thought of love, you will be drowned. If you give rise to a thought of anger, you will be buried. If you give rise to a thought of doubt, you will be bound. If you give rise to a thought of joy, you will be torn by the wind."

Such a philosophy can cause alienation from society. And a Zen idea like "All longing produces suffering" is difficult for the average person to accept. That is a wounded person's idea.

Meditate on the Zen ideas and follow those that give you a greater self-knowledge and a relaxed, content attitude. Don't follow ideas that alienate you and cause unpleasantness. Approach Zen not with skepticism but with patience and an open mind, and know in advance that it has limits.

Much of Zen is a very sensible, effective path to greater self-knowledge. Without accepting its extreme unreasonable doctrines, you can achieve more and better understand yourself and your motivation. Although you don't want it to disrupt the positive aspects of your place in society, the Zen approach to running can help you transcend the negative aspects of "normal" life in a personal, illuminating fashion.

CHAPTER EIGHT

RUNNING AND SPIRITUALISM

MANY OF THOSE WHOSE LIVES HAVE BEEN CHANGED BY running call it a spiritual activity. In fact, in the survey, 49 percent of the runners said that the euphoria they experienced on a run was sometimes "spiritual" in nature. Some credit the spiritual aspect of running with making their entire life-styles more positive.

Susan H., a Los Angeles runner, described the profound spiritual sensation that may be felt on a run: "I sometimes feel a true spiritual oneness while running. I feel a communication with the grass, the trees, other people, and with God."

These effects will occur if you let them, if you want them to be there, and if you are properly relaxed and understand meditative running. Many runners speak of individual, profound religious sensations similar to the glowing effect described in the last chapter. For others there isn't a single profound experience, but rather a gradual tendency toward spiritual enlightenment, a steady growth toward spiritualism.

Many go so far as to use religious terminology in describing their running experience. George Sheehan, for instance, who rediscovered running at age forty-five after being away from it for a couple of decades, said, "It was a decision that meant no less than a new life, a new course, a new destination. I was born again in my forty-fifth year."

And actor Ed Asner, who lost forty pounds and a lot of negativity through running, said, "I don't know if I was born again in the religious sense, but anything that makes you feel so alive has to become at least addictive, if not religious."

Reports of the spiritual sensation vary greatly. There is some debate whether these sensations are psychological or supernatural. And, of course, there are skeptics who say that such spiritual sensations don't happen at all. While compiling information for this book, I received this letter: "I've been running for fourteen years and have *never* had a 'religious' or 'euphoric' experience while running. Please don't write a so-called book on this subject."

This would seem to prove that you can approach exercise with a closed mind and still continue with it. But you miss a lot that way.

MIRACLES AND MYSTERIES

Among the 49 percent of the runners polled who sometimes get a spiritual sensation while running, the intensity certainly varies. One Missouri runner said he felt it so deeply that he seemed to be carried along by some force that "seemed wonderful, heavenly, or supernatural."

These spiritual enlightenments are supernatural in the

sense that they are unexplained; the American Heritage Dictionary defines supernatural as "not attributable to natural forces." This is the special sensation a runner may experience when he feels a religious sense of rightness and there is nothing tangible to which he can attribute the sensation.

The mysterious and miraculous running experience, which frees you from subconscious bonds, will only come when you have cleared your mind, at least temporarily, of scientific concepts. Scientific thinking strives to explain the unexplainable.

This is a problem that permeates all of society. The advancements of science have changed our perceptions and made us more skeptical. Once, there were emotional reasons for everything—lightning and rain happened because the gods were angry. Mankind worshiped idols, rocks, and paintings. But as science began to explain phenomena such as rain and thunder and fire, the unknown became less fanciful. We learned not to believe in ideas without having a scientific basis for our belief. We learned the reasons for being as we are; we learned about atoms and weather patterns and planets and galaxies and bloodstreams. But though scientific thought explains processes, it still doesn't answer the question of our existence.

Scientific thought has changed us. Rather than accept anything unexplainable, we tend to assume the explanation will appear eventually. This way mysteries disappear. It is scientific and cynical thinking that prevents the breakthroughs in running. Your mind must be relaxed and ready.

Dean A., a runner from Asbury Park, New Jersey, sums this up simply: "At first I didn't enjoy it a lot, but now

I'm more relaxed and I take a free, unstructured approach to running."

If half of the runners find it spiritual at times, this indicates that there is much to the running sensation that isn't easily explainable.

The glowing sensation described in the last chapter may be a characteristic of the spiritual experience. A respondent on the survey, from Long Beach, California, talked of this same effect in terms of spiritualism: "Sometimes when I'm in the right state of mind I'll get this unusual effect where everything seems to have a special kind of radiance. It's when I'm alone and I'm really up after I read a good book or have a great talk with someone, and everything seems so positive. Then sometimes I see this kind of radiance around everything. It's weird. It seems a little spiritual to me."

Many runners have these sensations, which might be called supernatural simply because they can't be explained or predicted. I tried to consciously recapture the glowing sensation mentioned in the previous chapter several times by recreating the circumstances that led up to it, before learning that the attempt to recreate it is itself a preventing factor. It won't happen through conscious attempt. That is why that experience is supernatural; I don't know why it happened.

The supernatural, wrote John Taylor in his book, *The Superminds*, "is equivalent to saying that the event in question cannot be explained in terms of natural processes, that is, in terms of a coherent set of events which have a clear causal relationship to one another."

The supernatural has probably touched us all, but we seldom accept it. We try to seek out causes for the unexplainable, to theorize explanations. This leads many to believe, without a factual basis, that nothing is really unexplainable. As Taylor wrote:

> A miracle can only stay miraculous if it remains uninvestigatable. If its secrets become exposed under the penetrating gaze of science, its supernatural character will go. Very few miracles have been accessible to investigation and even fewer stood up to scientific analysis. Perhaps it will come about that only the miracles of the past will preserve their mystery. Every so-called miracle is a challenge to science. . . . Will it ever turn out that the miracles of Jesus Christ also dissolve in scientific explanations?

Runners find that analysis of a euphoria only prevents it from happening again.

Olympic marathoner Don Kardong points out that "the scientist sees limits, the artist sees no limits." Kardong also speaks of "magical transformations" in his running. The supernatural running state will have nothing to do with witches or warlocks, but will open you up to the mysteries and miracles that lie beyond the scientific barriers of your mind. When you dig into the mysteries of the spiritual running experience, you are digging into your subconscious, not into vague spiritual ideas. It's all very real.

HOW RUNNING IS SPIRITUAL—
FIVE EXAMPLES

How does a form of exercise, something that makes you sweat and feel tired, become spiritual? Few people say there is anything spiritual about doing sit-ups or push-ups, and yet with running, just about half of those polled said they sometimes experience a spiritual euphoria. Many others say it gives them a more uniform spiritual state of mind. How does the "connection with God," as one runner put it, occur during this exercise? What is the experience like? Five respondents on the survey offered their descriptions.

"When I began running," wrote Diane B. of Iowa, "I had to wonder if I'd keep it up." Like many people who have taken up running in the last two years, she began it as an exercise, a way to lose a few pounds and get in better shape. When she started, she didn't expect it would ever become a religious sensation. "It was another thing to do each day. But my inclination to quit was a learned response, similar to the way I'd react to trying anything new, I suppose. I say this because as I sat afterward on my patio I'd realize how good it felt. Why did I think of quitting? I enjoyed this. It was so refreshing. Eventually, I enjoyed it and accepted the feeling so much that I *wanted* to run each day. It was an important thing for me. My husband thought I was crazy, but sometimes I even ran twice a day, it felt so good.

"I think running is religious, and I started thinking this well before I'd read any article about it in *Runner's World* or anyplace else. I remember the first time I thought it I was running on this gravel road through the middle of these fields of cows. There was no civilization to speak of anywhere I looked. I sort of started watching the cows and imagining it's just me and them. And then suddenly I just felt it and I thought, 'Well, here we are.' And it was a simple but real powerful realization. I think of it as religious because it's so natural and there's no way you can transfer in words the feeling of oneness you get. You're out there on your own accord, there's no requirement involved. It has absolutely nothing to do with your work or your obligations or the things you are expected to do. In fact, in the context of our purpose as it is dictated by the culture, running alone with a bunch of cows is ridiculous. But that's just why it's religious. It's so hard to explain it. It's such a private experience. I'm the only one out there with all those cows and that alone makes it an intensely personal event. The fact that there is nothing expected of me, that I'm open and free, and it feels so positive and important. That is religious."

Another description of the spiritual connection was offered by a Eugene, Oregon, runner who has run at least thirty miles a week every week since October of 1970: "I don't go to church on Sundays because I've always thought that religion shouldn't be found at a congregation. You've got to find it out for yourself. A lot of the people who go to church aren't finding out anything. I've always believed that religion was a personal commitment. I have to be alone to ever feel really religious. I get more out of an early morning run than I ever did from a church service. At church, you feel good and you get inspired, but it's the same way a coach gives a pep talk. It fades. On a run early in the morning, I get a realer feeling. I feel all that is real and true in the world. Runners know what I'm talking about. Before the cars have come out, when there's still dew on the grass and it's cool and crisp and you're out there all by yourself and you can see your breath. You just know. It's realer than anything else you can do in this life."

A more specific example was offered by Oxnard, California, runner Kenneth D., who began running in the summer of 1977 and admits he was skeptical of the talk of euphoria for "almost a full six and a half days."

"The term spiritual is appropriate to what might happen on a particularly good run," he said, "although some who have not experienced it might think it blasphemous to use it in this connection. But I've found that running can make you see the light. When I run while I'm depressed I get one of two reactions. I either feel lousy and want it to end or else I get this feeling that I'll describe as spiritual. I have to be relaxed but alert and tell myself I have nothing really to be depressed about. And then sometimes I'll see a sunset and it'll seem so clear that I'll think it's a message from God that, hey, everything's all right. It's so valuable it must be spiritual."

A less concrete explanation was given by this Greenville, Maine, runner of two years.

"Spiritual in nature? If you do it right it's much more than that. You feel all the beauty of the universe, you know the right of God's land. You know at that moment just why you were put here on this planet and what the purpose is of your life. The meaning of the stars, the sun, the highways all become clear. You sense that there is no evil in the world outside of your imagination. You know and feel everything. But after you've stopped running, you give that back, unfortunately, and return to your regular life, and you can't really know again until the next time you're out there running."

And finally, a New Jersey policeman, who began running several years ago to lose weight and only recently discovered the mental rewards, explained his own belief in the spiritual properties of running.

RUNNING AND SPIRITUALISM

"This question interests me, because I've sometimes thought of a few of my runs as being tranquil and maybe even a little bit religious. I'm anxious to see what the other runners say. For me, it sometimes is very peaceful and makes me feel at peace with the world. If I'm all tense at the end of a day, as I sometimes am, the run calms me and puts me where I should be. I do all my running at night, usually after it's become dark. I wouldn't want to run any other time. Nighttime is just right for putting me in the frame of mind I'm talking about. It's pretty quiet by where I live and the streets are pretty deserted after about six o'clock and it feels good to go out there. I see all the families in their houses eating dinner or watching TV and there are kids out playing still and I get a feeling of calmness as if there is a wonderful order to everything. Is that spiritual?"

HOW RUNNING CAN BECOME MYSTICAL

Running can be a mystical activity if the runner has a unique state of mind. The meditation and Zen ideas of the preceding chapters ready the runner for this stage.

A number of runners have talked of running as a mystical activity. "A mystical unity" is created, one magazine article mentioned. One respondent on the survey said that "Sometimes running seems mystical in nature."

Four steps can be identified in creating a state of mind conducive to a spiritual outlook:

1. Clear your mind of negative or nagging thoughts. Try to keep it clear as in meditation.

2. Concentrate on relaxing and clearing tensions from your body and mind.

3. Think humble, as if you are a creature running, not unlike a cat or a dog.

4. Pay attention, in a meditative fashion, to the grass, the trees, the sky, i.e. nature, your physical surroundings.

The spiritual state of mind is more difficult to reach than the meditative state of mind mostly because it is more vague; it is intuitive and requires a suspension of preoccupations.

Webster defines mysticism as both "a vague speculation" and "the doctrine or belief that direct knowledge of God, of spiritual truth, of ultimate reality, or comparable matters is attainable through immediate intuition, insight or illumination and in a way differing from ordinary sense perception." Runners have to open their minds to intuition and reject the formal barriers that normally restrict their thinking.

"When I have an unusual mental experience running," explained a Lompoc, California, runner, "it generally stems from just letting go and not worrying about things. For example, last May when I got out of school after my last final, I went on a run and there was this great weight relieved from my back and I just didn't have any obligations or plans or anything and I let myself go, and I felt in an odd way like I was communicating with nature, that I grasped this great importance in the grass and trees. I was suddenly released from all of this inward thinking that I'd been doing during school and suddenly I was a part of nature. It's amazing, it happens when there's all this great weight lifted off your back, like finishing school or finishing a project or winning something."

The mystical experience is deeply rooted in the subconscious; it is an opening of doors of emotion and joy.

One additional requirement for being able to experience the mystical sensation is that you have in mind some concept of the rightness of the world, even if it is subconscious. If you have accepted the Zen philosophy, this should occur naturally. The concept I'm speaking of can be religious, personal, or Zen-like. Then, when you have a relaxed state of mind, the mystical sensation can happen fairly often as you run.

"Mysticism arises when ideas which have hardened into formal worship and doctrine are transformed into purely personal and inward experience," wrote Geoffrey Nelson in his book, *Spiritualism and Society.*

The point is that the mystical state of mind can be reached; it is intuitive and a bit vague, but it is also deeply personal and very real to those who experience it.

PURITY

Making running a total activity and obliterating goals in the process can be interpreted as a religious concept. Wrote Reinhold Niebuhr, "Religion seeks to persuade men to sacrifice immediate advantages for ultimate values." This is what happens as running becomes a total inner-directed activity.

Richard P., of Wawatosa, Wisconsin, is a devout Christian and a strong believer in the relationship between running and Christianity. He cites several biblical references to running and believes that running is a very religious activity. And he feels that the healing properties of running are Christian.

"I can tell you it's been great. You probably know how much we are just beginning to learn about psychosomatic illness. So much goes back to the mind. Whether it's pain, fatigue, or even injury. Consider what God says to the runner. In my athletic experience, it's all true."

The progression of running, beyond Zen and meditation, is toward becoming purer.

"I've been able to develop a deep, warm religious feeling when I go out on a run early in the morning," wrote a Connecticut runner. "It's a feeling of certainty, love, knowledge, and religion. It's true and it's peaceful and is the best direction I now have through my days."

With or without the acceptance of religious ideas or terminology, as the runner becomes purer, his mind becomes more relaxed; as he achieves enlightenment, he becomes more religious.

INFORMAL RELIGION

Runners who talk of running as a religion almost always mention the personal and unorganized aspects of it. Religious experiences most often occur to runners while they are running alone rather than when running with friends or at a weekend road race.

The earlier example of the runner who said he gets more out of a morning run alone than a weekly church meeting explains the special aspect of running that can make it spiritual. Most people simply don't look for religion in unorthodox personal means. Sometimes they accept formal religion without a true commitment or understanding.

Said Niebuhr, "The old challenge 'be ye not conformed to this world' must be accepted anew in a more heroic fashion than is customary in religious circles."

Those who find a spiritual side to running are those who *feel it*, who have broken through the rigidity of their thinking and accept religion in a true but informal manner, rather than in a conforming and formal way.

Spiritualism is an active religious idea directed toward greater personal understanding and enlightenment. It is, as Geoffrey Nelson wrote in *Spiritualism and Society*, "mainly a personal religion based on the experience of its members and existing primarily for their individual needs."

ABSTRACTIONS

Initially, the effects of running are very concrete—you feel a shortness of breath, a soreness in your legs, you feel better or worse about yourself, you lose a little weight.

Then, as you continue to develop through Total Running, the feelings and reasons for running become less concrete. Some never reach the more profound sensations because they demand concrete definitions for what they experience. In order for the inner transformation to take place, the concrete way of thinking must be at least temporarily sacrificed.

The most intense sensations are those that are most abstract. They are all possible, though, if the runner accepts nonlogical feeling rather than explanations—the trance-like experience of meditation, the purity of action cultivated through Zen, the euphorias of enlightenment, the "glowing" sensation.

Freedom of intuition is the key to spiritual running. You run as you feel, and the meaning and specific effects of running become less easy to communicate. The earlier, concrete effects—weight loss and so forth—are now taken for granted. This is the progression which this book is about, the progression toward Total Running. Follow logic until you know what it is you are doing and then proceed on your intuition.

THE PUZZLE

Many people refrain from totally devoting themselves to a religious idea because they feel the choice is too simple and too easy. They suspect that the matter of our existence is much more complicated—something to which they will give attention throughout their lives, though mostly in idle moments. They prefer working on a puzzle with no guaranteed solution to committing themselves to belief in any doctrine or religious idea.

Unfortunately, the puzzle is probably not solvable. Many prefer it anyway because they feel you are constantly learning about yourself, whereas if you've accepted a religion, you stop evolving in some essential ways.

With inner-directed Total Running you do learn about yourself, but you don't try to solve futile puzzles. This is the Zen way of enlightenment: saying there are no puzzles rather than trying to solve them.

For example, a runner from Evanston, Illinois, says she became euphoric through a process of realizing that nothing was really complicated: "My experience was one of becoming more in touch with my life and my direction. I treasured the time I was on a run because it was so pure and it dissolved worries in my mind that built up during the day. I feel better all the time."

Running as spiritualism is the lifting from your shoulders of an insoluble puzzle. This is the spiritual elation of which runners speak.

CHAPTER NINE

RUNNING AND THE ASTRAL SENSATION

FOR THE PAST TWO DECADES, INTEREST HAS BEEN GROWing in "out-of-body experiences" (OBEs) and psychic phenomena in general. The deep state of relaxation that can be developed through Total Running seems particularly conducive to the out-of-body experience.

Although the mention of astral sensations might conjure images of 1950's science fiction movies, the OBE has been clinically researched for nearly a hundred years now. A number of researchers have devoted their lives to the study of this psychic phenomenon.

The astral experience was something Freud and Jung debated. Plutarch wrote of an unconscious soldier who wandered in another dimension for several days before returning to his physical body. The great French writer de Maupassant claimed to have been in a depressed and tense state of mind once when his astral double entered the room where he was writing and began dictating to him. A number of African tribes still practice rituals to separate the soul from the physical body.

The state of mind believed necessary for an astral projection is not easily achieved. It generally occurs only in cases of extreme tension or extreme relaxation. As a runner's mental outlook evolves from exercise to relaxation to meditation to Zen, this extreme relaxation is possible.

Many runners report experiences that can be defined as psychic, including astral experiences. Because it can put the mind in a relaxed, almost hypnotic state, running seems very conducive to the astral sensation. Of course, a runner must also overcome skepticism and accept the possibility of profound, perhaps unexplainable experience.

Out-of-body experiences, whether they are psychological manifestations or are actually a separation of body and soul, can occur if a runner lets them happen. Such experiences may only be illusions, or they may be actual events. Either way, the OBE will be thought-provoking and will lead to new insights.

WHAT IS AN ASTRAL SENSATION?

The astral or out-of-body experience is a sensation in which a person first feels as if he is floating and then has a momentary blacking out as his "spirit" rises from his body. Specifics vary greatly. A separation, whether real or imagined, occurs between the soul and the physical body. A double, called the "astral body" or "astral double," is projected. Many researchers believe that the astral double has a real existence, electromagnetic or electrical in nature. In fact, in the book *Journeys Out of the Body*, Robert Monroe described experiencing his astral double traveling over telephone lines. It is often reported that during the

150

astral sensation the physical body is motionless and without consciousness and that a cord exists connecting the physical and astral bodies.

The factors most often responsible for returning the astral body to the physical body are fear, worry, or loud noise. The nature of the experience and its specific manifestations vary. "The double may move in various ways," wrote Herbert Greenhouse in *The Astral Journey*, "walk, glide, float, fly—it may stay near the physical body or travel great distances at lightning speed . . . it may range from just a wispy presence to a very solid 3-D body that walks, talks and breathes exactly as a physical body."

Parapsychologists and psychic researchers believe that astral projections are based on a subconscious need or anxiety. Sometimes when the physical body is in threat of injury or great pain, the astral projection will occur. Many sensations are reported during accidents or in war situations. The person becomes detached and actually sees his physical body in danger. Some even say that their astral projection has been able to save their physical body by moving it out of the way of further damage.

Sometimes the astral experience is telepathic in nature or the astral body seeks to communicate with another person, sometimes someone the physical person hasn't seen in years. But the most common time for the astral occurrence is during sleep. Some believe all dreams are an astral experience and others think that sleep itself is an astral sensation. "What causes sleep," wrote Pierre-Émile Cornillier in *The Survival of the Soul*, "is a disunion between the astral body and the physical body."

Many say they have seen the astral bodies of others while

some claim the astral body is visible only to themselves. "There are two kinds of astral mind-over-matter," wrote Greenhouse.

In one, physical objects prove no barrier to the second body, which can pass right through them. The other kind . . . occurs when the double can create sounds, handle and move material objects and make physical contact with people . . . Generally, projectors who have the one kind of mind-over-matter ability are not capable of the other.

An altered state of mind is necessary before the astral sensation will happen. Many authors on the subject speak of the importance of performing a rhythmic activity for a sustained amount of time in order for this to occur. Common examples include typing, walking, chanting, singing, and running.

AN EXAMPLE

Brent S. is a runner from Brooklyn, New York. One night last year, as he was cooling off after a five-mile run, something peculiar happened. He had experienced a floating feeling over the final laps of his run. As he walked around the track during his cool-down the floating feeling became more intense. He lay down on the grass as it continued and then "my running spirit disengaged itself from my encasing [the body]." Then he says his astral body ran a lap around the track as he lay in the grass.

Consistent with most accounts of the OBE, he temporarily blacked out when the astral body left his physical

body, "lift off," as he put it. "I had not one iota of consciousness at lift-off." But inconsistent with most traditional accounts, he was able to perceive his astral body from
his physical body. Usually people claim it is the other way
around.

"It happened after the run," Brent explained. "It started
during the end of the run. I can't really simplify it any
more than it seems.

"I believe it happened for the simple reason that I
believed it could. I've had an OBE while sleeping and I
know it happens. This particular OBE, as with the one
during my sleep, was not intentional."

During the one in his sleep the situation was different,
as he had consciousness in his astral body rather than in
his physical body. He's still experimenting with the psychic
experience.

"I've tried to explain it to myself many times," said
Brent, "and the closest I've come to an explanation is that
it's not any special feat. I believe we all have the power
to make all of our 'systems go.' "

Although he does think it's a natural process, he thinks
it can be sought just by reaching a relaxed "all systems go"
state of mind.

"I have not tried to make it happen again yet for the
reason that the days have been going by so fast and I've
been training for the New York Marathon. I did not direct
my energies toward the projection itself. But now I will
start trying.

"It's as simple as it sounds, and that's the way it happened. I hope it will be again. It is an enlightening you
never want to forget."

HOW DOES IT FEEL?

Some who've experienced the astral sensation say their astral self feels no different from their physical self. More common is a description of lightness and painlessness. This seems to be the state that runners approach during their euphoria (which 78 percent of the runners I polled say they experience at least on occasion).

Some believe that the astral body allows a feeling of omnipotence and perfection. This too is similar to the feeling many runners get from their running. As Boulder, Colorado, runner Carl S. said, "I get a feeling of transcending all time and space from my running."

Although the astral experience has a profound effect, as with all mental and psychic phenomena, it can never be explained as intensely as it is felt. And this too is in accordance with peak running experiences.

FLOATING

Although accounts of astral sensations while running as dramatic as Brent S.'s aren't common, many speak of what he described as the prelude to his astral experience: the sensation of floating. I have known it as an effortless feeling where there is no discomfort and almost no sensation of the physical action of running. This condition is clearly an intended result of integrating meditation, Zen, and spiritual ideas with running and is reached after one is able to achieve a state of extreme relaxation.

One explanation of the floating sensation was offered by Fort Worth, Texas, runner Marvin C.: "The only euphoric feeling I get is this floating feeling, usually about three-fourths of the way through a run. I get it usually about two or three times a week; sometimes, though, if I'm not in a good mood, it might not happen for a couple of weeks. It makes all my bad runs worth it. I can never really tell when I start a run if it's going to happen this time, though I do think about it. About halfway through if it's going to happen I feel very smooth and good, I won't be worrying about drivers giving me a hard time or feel any uncomfortableness in my legs. The run'll just start getting easier from that point. I won't have any thoughts about ending it or how long I've been running and I'll just like the fact that I'm running. I like it more and more. I like everything about it and feel that nothing can annoy me. And then I'm suddenly in this amazing state where everything is perfect and I'm almost literally floating. I'm not running. There's no effort involved. I can't feel my legs moving. It's just a wonderful feeling. I'd say it generally lasts for about five minutes, although sometimes if I'm running through a real scenic spot it could last longer, like fifteen minutes."

Creating the relaxed attitude and going with the feeling is what leads to the psychic experiences. You have to first clear your mind of external problems. Presumably, by the time you have reached this point in the book you are able to do that.

THE REASONS FOR PROJECTION

Those who've studied astral phenomena seem in agreement that the projections generally have a purpose. Often this reason is a suppressed personality conflict. Other times, the reason is obvious. It may be a protection against physical pain. "The double is often forcibly ejected from the body when there is a threat of sudden death or painful injury," wrote Pierre-Émile Cornillier. "It happens also when pain and suffering become so intense they can no longer be endured." But it may also happen for less serious reasons. Many theorize that nagging worries and mild anxieties are exorcised by the astral experience.

In *The Phenomena of Astral Projection* authors Muldoon and Carrington described the projection of a German woman who one day was taking a nap because she had a bad headache. She woke up and felt very light; her headache was suddenly gone. She followed her mother down a hallway into the living room and watched her as she sat and began knitting while her father read aloud from a book. She was surprised that they didn't acknowledge her presence. When she went back to her own room she knew why. She saw her physical body sleeping "pale and corpse-like." And it was at that moment of realization that the two bodies merged.

Sometimes the astral projection seems to occur because of a subconscious wish or need to communicate with another person. Some claim that they have telepathic communication and this creates a psychic bond. This bond begins, generally, with an emotional bond.

One runner on the survey spoke of such a bond he had with his girl friend: "My girl friend Kim and I really believe we have telepathy. It's unbelievable how well we know what the other is thinking. Running seems a perfect activity for this. When we're on a run we communicate mentally without speaking. We know what each other is thinking and seeing, we even know when the other one wants to stop or to turn around. I don't know why it seems to happen especially on a run, but it does."

Sometimes the reason for an astral experience isn't very apparent even after the experience has been studied. Psychics who claim to have astral projections regularly say that the reason, although they believe it exists, is so submerged that an analysis of the experience won't yield it.

The purpose for an astral projection doesn't have to be a matter of life or death. It might be very simple. As Herbert Greenhouse wrote:

> We have seen how the conscience of a clerk propelled him back to his dry goods shop during his lunch hour, how a businessman rose in his double from a sickbed and met the salesman he was unable to contact in his physical body. . . . Even something as prosaic as getting home in time for dinner may release the astral body ahead of the physical body.

Precisely why an astral projection happens at the times when it does and not at others is unknown, although an altered state of mind must precede it.

HOW TO HAVE AN ASTRAL SENSATION

The best means of achieving an astral experience is by being in an altered state of mind—either extremely tense or extremely relaxed. The extremely tense mind is a dangerous condition, but the very relaxed mind is what this book has been working toward. Cultivation of relaxation and a willingness to allow unexplainable sensations to occur are the primary prerequisites. Time of day and temperament immediately before the run are also factors.

Through the meditation exercises and Zen awareness, you should be able to develop a state of mind cleared of extraneous thought and conducive to psychic experience. Generally, these experiences won't occur while you're thinking about what groceries you have to buy or if you're worrying about whether or not you paid your last phone bill.

The OBE shouldn't be forced. It should evolve naturally from a state of relaxation. Most authorities on the subject agree on two points: the astral experience cannot be forced, and it occurs most frequently during sleep or in unnatural states of mind.

Robert Crookall, an Englishman in his eighties who has written thirteen books on the astral experience, says that there should never be any deliberate attempts to hasten the experience. Rather, it should be a natural process that occurs when a person is in the proper state of mind. The same thing is true of altered and psychic states of mind reached through running. It shouldn't be a purposely sought-after sensation, but rather a natural occurrence through an evolution of attitude.

PSYCHIC EXPERIENCE AND RUNNING

Besides the astral experience, there are a number of feelings and perceptions runners have that can only be described as psychic. Sometimes, particularly among new runners, these can be related to deep urges and conflicts that might have been festering in the subconscious for years. It is the active, unique state of mind developed through running that causes this.

Spiritual and Zen enlightenments are clearer than psychic experiences; they seem to offer answers to the questions of our existence; they are a feeling of "rightness." Psychic experiences are less uniform. The spiritual sensation often pertains to God and our existence. The psychic sensation, which includes telepathy, ESP, and astral sensations, is more symbolic.

In her book *The Psychic Power of Running*, Valerie Andrews ventured this esoteric explanation of the psychic running experience: "We are going back in time to images that were once invoked by priests and shamans, early practitioners of healing who knew that transformation did not occur on the intellectual plane but required a transference of physical and psychic energy."

John W., of Van Nuys, California, related this example of a psychic running experience: "It's a communication with forces I don't exactly understand. It's like a feeling of ESP with other runners. I think a lot of people get this but don't admit it. It's strong, like my mind is in another plane of existence."

Many runners mention the phenomenon of apparent displacement in time and space. This is how the psychic experience begins. A long-term Zen-like approach to running can produce this feeling of displacement fairly regularly and perhaps lead to the psychic states beyond it.

Dane L., a runner from San Rafael, California, explained the subtle way in which the psychic sensation is approached;

he calls it the "Zone." What he says is universal: psychic experiences must be reached through practicing the development of a state of mind.

"I've been learning to run more and more in what I call the 'Zone.' I can now tune into this space and find it by allowing myself to mentally and physically shift gears to a smooth, effortless stride. I become so simple-minded or concentrated or no-minded in my attention of flowing in the 'Zone' that a magical transformation seems to take place that allows me to flow through the universe with an awareness that extends beyond my body/mind connection. Sometimes, I can get to this space in three or four runs a week."

ASTRAL EXPERIENCE AND CHILDHOOD

As has been pointed out, the successful development of Total Running in many ways involves becoming more childlike in perception. When barriers of adult thinking are broken through, a truer means of perception is attained. This is a goal of the relaxation and meditation exercises.

The childhood state of mind is especially relevant to the astral experience and psychic phenomena in general. Parapsychologists believe children have the most frequent psychic experiences, although they sometimes don't realize them as such. In his book *Superminds,* John Taylor reported a study done on children's and adults' abilities to bend metal just by concentration. The study divided people with this power into three groups based on the extent of their ability. Of the thirty-eight people in the advanced

category, all but four were under seventeen years of age.
Fourteen were boys, twenty were girls. Seven of the children
were severely retarded.

"It is interesting to note," Taylor wrote, "the almost
complete absence of adult males on this list; excluding Uri
Geller, only *one* case is known of a male over twenty years
old possessing this power. Against this, there is the high
proportion of children."

No research has been done on whether children are more
likely than adults to have astral sensations during or after
a run. The survey I made was almost entirely composed of
adults. But from personal experience, I believe that the
profound euphorias and unusual mental experiences are
more easily attained when you are younger, though when
you attain them as an adult, they are probably more profound.

Adult thinking is more orderly than childhood thinking
—often too orderly. While gaining this order, we sometimes lose our sense of possibility, of creativity.

One runner from Louisiana explained the reversion in
thinking: "After I'd been running for a few months, I became more vibrant in my thinking, I was more enthused
about things, had more spunk. It was almost as if I had become a child again."

The process of breaking down stringent adult barriers
of thinking leads to greater imagination and, within limits,
fantasy. It is also the process for psychic and astral experience.

"To young children," wrote Herbert Greenhouse, "fantasy, sometimes the fantasy of flying, becomes merged with
reality. They are rarely surprised when they find themselves

out of their physical bodies and floating around delightfully in their astral vehicles."

ILLUSION OR REALITY?

Possibly all astral sensation can be explained as imagination, as images from the subconscious. But we have no real way of knowing.

Evelyn W. of Boston has several times projected herself running with friends she hasn't seen in years. Once, while running through the streets of Boston, she says she was transported to Paris, France. But she believes the experiences were more imagination than spiritualism.

"I'm sure there was a logical explanation," she said. "I've got an active imagination anyway, so when I start thinking about an old friend, it isn't so unnatural to imagine myself running with her again. But there are moments when I have to wonder; there are times my imagination surprises me. The time I seemed to be transported to Paris was especially like this. I'd been to Paris for two weeks four and a half years before, but hadn't really thought of it consciously a whole lot, but suddenly, while I was running in Boston, I turned a corner and there I was on this street in Paris where I'd stayed. Every detail was there—all the shops, the cracks in the sidewalk, the street, the signs. It took a few seconds until I was not there, until I was back on that street in Boston where I was really running. But the point is, for those few instants, I *was* in Paris."

Sometimes the person who has an astral or psychic sensation will know it is the product of an active imagination.

Other times, though, he won't know this but will simply rationalize it as such.

Parapsychologists acknowledge that there are, indeed, imagined, illusory OBEs, but they draw a distinction between these and actual astral sensations.

Said Herbert Greenhouse, "If one concedes that psychological and physical abnormalities such as brain damage sometimes bring on the illusion of the double, it does not follow that all OBEs are hallucinations. Wouldn't it be more to the point to say that because so many normal persons have OBEs, those in abnormal states may also be having them? It is becoming increasingly evident that the psychic experiences, OBEs or others . . . can happen to anyone, the healthy-minded as well as the mentally disturbed."

Still, OBEs don't happen to everyone with the same ease. Sensitivity and emotion seem to be significant factors.

There are some people who naturally are more emotional than others, and for them the astral sensation is more likely to occur than for a more logical thinker, mostly because they are mentally more open to it. But if the more logically minded person has such an experience it will undoubtedly be more profound, because it will be so unlike the rest of his thinking.

Those who experience psychic phenomena are often more emotional, but this could support either side of the question. It could indicate that they are more prone to make up such episodes, or it might indicate that they have broken through the barriers of rigid thinking and are thus more ready for a real psychic experience. Some believe, in fact, that the OBE is an extension of emotion. Arthur

163

Conan Doyle wrote, in *The Edge of the Unknown,* "If a sensitive person is able to feel some record of a past event, then there is evidence that by an extension of this process one who is still more sensitive would actually see the person who left the impression."

So what should be striven for, and embraced when it begins to happen, is the deepening of sensitivity into a positive, relaxed state of mind, open to unexplainable experience.

When this happens, psychic phenomena and the astral experience are possible.

164

CHAPTER TEN

RUNNING AND THE FOUNTAIN OF YOUTH

THE AGING PROCESS IS AMONG THE CHIEF PRODUCERS OF anxiety in contemporary life. Throughout history, we have searched for ways of lessening or avoiding it. But we remain at the mercy of this inevitable fact of life, and often our worry and fear over it only hasten the whole process.

A new attitude about aging is the logical conclusion to the evolution of mental outlook developed in this book. The ultimate aspect of Total Running is transcending your fears of aging. You become less rigid in your thinking and are able to naturally experience the same joyful emotions that you did in childhood.

"Running brings a person back to his youth," wrote Joanne D., an Ardmore, Pennsylvania, runner. "It makes you feel young, keeps you in touch with nature and close to the earth, makes you appreciate all that is truly beautiful."

RUNNING AND AGING

Science, we are told, is on the verge of substantially prolonging the average lifespan. A 1964 survey by the Rand Corporation in Santa Monica, California, of eighty-two of the world's top gerontologists revealed that most agreed that the average life expectancy would be twenty years greater by the 1990's. More recently, scientist Durk Pearson has been telling talk show audiences that it's not inconceivable that science will be able to prolong the average lifespan 100 or more years within the century. The practice of freezing people, cryogenics, gained recognition in the sixties, and there are now more than fifty people in the United States whose bodies have been frozen. Gerontologist Alex Comfort has said, "If the scientific and medical resources of the United States alone were mobilized, aging could be conquered by something not unlike the fountain of youth Ponce de León searched for."

Exercise is clearly one of the ways in which we can prolong life. Running strengthens the heart and helps prevent heart attacks. It also eases tension, prevents cholesterol levels from building, and lowers blood pressure.

Alexander Leaf of the Harvard Medical School states, "Exercise is the closest thing to an antiaging pill." And Dr. Hans Kugler of Roosevelt University in Chicago says that exercise slows aging and can add six to nine years to the average life expectancy.

But we're talking only about statistics, the physiological basis of aging. The mental element is much less easy to quantify, though it is certainly significant. What is it that accounts for two men of the same age and similar life-styles appearing to be ten or twenty years apart?

Our attitudes and our personality do have a control over how fast our bodies age. As Laurence Morehouse, founding director of UCLA's Human Performance Laboratory, said, "While chronological age is invariable, physiological age has a variable of thirty years. Suppose you are fifty. You can have the outward appearance and internal system of a sixty-five-year-old or a thirty-five-year-old. It's entirely up to you. An inactive life is a slow form of suicide. The right kind of exercise buys years."

One's mental growth has a great deal to do with aging, and that is what this book is concerned with. A proper attitude and approach to living has an immeasurable effect on longevity.

Recently, Dr. Robert Samp of the University of Wisconsin studied two thousand elderly people and determined that longevity depended on the following personality traits: moderation, serenity, optimism, interest in other people, and an interest in the future.

And studies of the world's longest-living people—those between the Black and Caspian seas in the Soviet Union—reveal that these same traits are found there as well as a great deal of natural, relaxed exercise.

Developing a relaxed attitude and new ideas is as important in retarding the aging process as is proper nutrition. Accordingly, because it combines the benefits of relaxation with the age-deterring benefits of physical exercise, Total Running, as a lifelong commitment, is one of the best means of staying young.

It is, finally, what we do with our life that determines

how much of it we have. You are young when you realize your potential and the possibilities of your life.

"He is born man, and he can't change that," wrote Stewart Edward White in *The Unobstructed Universe*,

but he is also born with a degree of quality individual to himself. This, too, he can never change—his capacity for doing, for understanding, for becoming. But he can fulfill that capacity; he can win for his individual consciousness a degree of quantitative development proportionate to his quality.

That is what running can do and, in so doing, that is how it can keep us young.

THE CHILD

The major barriers to becoming positively childlike are the worries, habits, and obligations that adults have but children never have. The transcendental aspect of Total Running enables you to lessen or escape these artificial boundaries to your life. You become free, at least momentarily, and in this sense you feel younger again. Many of the most intense running sensations involve the feelings of becoming younger.

"We all look for the secret of eternal youth," Leo Y., a fifty-four-year-old runner from Elizabeth, New Jersey, said. "To us runners, the young boy in us will never die."

Adults sometimes get a euphoric sensation just from doing what they did regularly as children, something as simple as lying out in the grassy backyard at twilight. Running works in a similar way. It simplifies. Regardless of how complicated the rest of a person's life might be, when he is on a run he is a creature, an animal pure and simple, moving. Many people forget this simple fact and suddenly realize it again only when they start running.

THE POETIC SEARCH

We aren't unlike Juan Ponce de León, the tired war veteran who was enticed by tales of an enchanted island in the Bahamas with an unlimited supply of gold and fruit and beautiful women and, at its center, a fountain with water that would make you eternally young. Early in the 1500's, he set out on his futile quest; he tasted virtually every fountain in the Bahamas and discovered Florida, but never found his fountain.

We too search the unknown, sometimes in a similarly ridiculous fashion, simply because we don't know the topography of where we're searching. And we, too, entertain magical ideas such as eternal youth and perfection. We can attain some satisfaction in this search just through attitude.

Probably we each have an image of ourselves that is at least a little different from what we are—a fantasy self. This fantasy self is the perfect person we could, and feel we should, be. He's a little more successful than us, a little more content, a little more confident maybe. He is immune to those petty problems, decisions, and habits that plague our real selves.

This alter ego is mentally and spiritually, if not physically, younger and in better shape. Running can bring us closer to him.

169

"I'm becoming more what I've long known I should be," said a Chattanooga, Tennessee runner.

When you are moving toward what you want to be, you seem to grow younger. That is the evolution of Total Running, that is the search we are concerned with.

DISCOVERING THE FOUNTAIN

Probably the most detailed and revealing response on the survey was from Debra J., from a suburb of Atlanta, who discovered running after being divorced and feeling much older than she was.

"When I got divorced, I felt like an old woman. I didn't want to go out. I just spent all of my time with the kids and at my job. I didn't want to start over or get involved in anything new. I believed I would never really feel young again. I thought that was all past. I loved my children, but there was something missing. It was more than just another person, it was a feeling of excitement. Nothing excited me.

"I tell you this because this is the way things were for me when I started running in the spring of 1976. One of my friends at the office could see I wasn't too happy, I guess, and she told me I should start jogging. She told me she'd lost eight pounds from it and felt a whole lot better herself. I always told her maybe, but it didn't really excite me. Then one day on a weekend she called me up and asked if I wanted to. I didn't really but I wanted to get out of the house so I said okay. I put on these old grocery-store tennis shoes I'd used while painting and a pair of cutoff shorts and a Disney World T-shirt. Not exactly the model running outfit. We went real slow, only about four or five blocks. I didn't like the jogging itself so much, but the conversation and just being outside with somebody felt real good. I'd been spending most of my weekends home watching the kids and watching TV. It made me feel a lot younger, too, like before I was married and I'd go and do things with my girl friends.

"So when my friend, Jeannette, asked me if I wanted to try again next weekend I said okay. I even told her I'd practice a little bit during the week. I never got around to practicing, but the next weekend we did it again and I went a lot farther. Afterward, she told me all about her running, how she ran every day, belonged to the AAU and ran races each weekend. That really got me, because she's about ten years older than me and married and has seven kids. It inspired me. I thought if she can do it I sure can. So I had her explain to me all about these races she ran and how I should get ready."

As with many who discover running at a point when their life seems stagnant, it brought a profound change to Debra's life.

"The main thing that happened was I became excited, and I hadn't been excited about anything since I'd been divorced. That was three years. I went out and bought all these things like books and shoes and running clothes. All these new things were really symbolic too. My kids couldn't understand what I was so excited about. They had no idea what had been going on in my mind for the past three years. When I got interested in running I thought I was a little afraid I might not be able to spend as much time with them, but the way it happened I wanted to spend more.

I felt closer to them and more able to talk with them. I'd been acting like this old woman for so long.

"Running set me on the right track. Jeannette took me to a fun-run and I ran the half mile. I really enjoyed the atmosphere. So I started going regularly. And I met a few people, two of whom I ran with sometimes after work. They were people like me. That was great to find out. They may have started running because they wanted to lose a few pounds, but they were here at the fun-runs because it felt good and they liked that sort of atmosphere of healthiness.

"I really improved fast, getting my half-mile times down. And I made some new friends, lost a little weight and most of all felt much better. All summer as I kept running I found myself becoming more outgoing. People noticed the change. Some of the people at work even complimented me on the way I'd changed. I'd feel so much energy sometimes I'd have to make myself keep my mind on my work. I enjoyed the work a bit more. Before, I'd just be glued to it but not really enjoying it."

By early 1977 she was so involved in running that she set her sights on running a marathon, the Peach Bowl race in January of 1978 in Atlanta. All through 1977 she thought of it and enjoyed herself training for it.

"I think 1977 must have been the best year of my life. I couldn't believe what I was doing, running all these miles. I felt really in with all these runners in the area. I started running local races. It was amazing. I also became much more happy at home. I'd come home from work, go out on a run and come back, make dinner and just be with my kids. They saw that I changed. I took a much greater interest in them, I even became childish sometimes with them and played with them. I'd never have done that before.

"I tell you all this because I hope people who are skeptical will see how positive running can be. I think a lot of skeptical people aren't really happy people. They just sit back and say that things aren't good. But they miss out on the things that are good. At first, I thought it was unnatural that I was running. Now I realize it was unnatural that I was so withdrawn for three years. Running got me out of that. That was unnatural. I didn't feel any joy for three years. Maybe some isolated moments of happiness, but no real joy. I don't think that should happen to anyone. I became afraid of joy. Believe me, I missed out on a lot. Now that I know what joy is again, my whole life has changed. Even now, people are telling me how much more alive I've become. I love it. I hope people realize it's possible. The only thing keeping you from what you want is yourself."

RUNNING AND PERSONAL HISTORY

Running is intricately tied up with the subconscious. Running makes you remember—not ideas so much as it makes you remember, even relive, feelings, similar to the way music or old photographs might. Running may respark old all-but-forgotten feelings and hopes. You may remember and re-experience precise feelings. It is different from sitting and thinking about old times. It is motion. It is, as with Zen, actually going out and experiencing the feelings again.

The best example of this from the survey was supplied by Torrance, California, runner Tyler D., who said, "Sometimes when I'm running, I'll slip into a weird mood where it seems like I'm at another point in my life. This is what a lot of people talk about when they say they forget all sense of time. Especially when I'm running at Christmas I get real strong vibes of past Christmases, all the emotions and everything. It doesn't happen while I'm walking and I'm not sure why it just happens while I'm running. Last year, I remember I went running at night and there were Christmas decorations up and I began remembering little things, like I suddenly remembered this ornament we used to have on our tree when I was a little kid and I began to remember how important that ornament had been to me and our family. I mean, it was really an emotional moment. And one time I just remembered one day I went shopping at a department store with my brother and we had cheeseburgers at the grill and bought this statue for my father. It was just one year but these are things I hadn't thought about in years, they'd been forgotten and all of a sudden I remembered them and not only that, I felt them again. It was very emotional."

The subconscious turns up forgotten gems like this when you are properly relaxed. Without the preconceptions and barriers of your life-style, your subconscious opens up and suppressed thoughts, feelings, and ideas that were once very deeply and emotionally felt can surface again. You are in all parts of your life; it is like the concept Kurt Vonnegut explained in *Slaughterhouse-Five*, that all time—past, present, and future—exists at once, if only in your memory.

When the positive, suppressed portions of your thought processes surface, this is when you can clear the psychological problems and worries from your mind and again accept some of what was once tangible, but had been suppressed perhaps since you were a child.

For many this means the return of magic. This magic can probably be found in other ways, but running has become a proven way. It can unlock doors of possibility, open up closed thinking and stifled life-styles.

As Valerie Andrews wrote in *The Psychic Power of Running*:

> You obtain a power charge that runs from the psychic core to the conscious level and evokes childhood memories, uncovers secret goals and unarticulated wishes, inspires vivid fantasies and dreams, and illuminates the interior framework of the soul, laying the foundation for far-reaching psychological change. This process is so powerful and unique that we need an entirely new set of suppositions about the origins of man in order to explain it.

PLAY

The goal of Total Running is to make the physical action of running a source of self-knowledge and enlightenment, but still fun. The enlightenment should come naturally; it should never be forced. When you've accepted and learned this, the process of enlightenment in itself is fun.

As a Los Angeles runner said, "I just enjoy it. Then you can talk about the cardiovascular and psychological benefits. Foremost, though, it's just something I enjoy."

Making running play-like is part of the evolution this

book deals with. Running may be a chore at first, but eventually it changes to something that you want to do that gives you something back. It is, at root, a healthy, relaxing and introspective form of play.

The return to play, which is often sacrificed from our life-styles during the process of becoming adult, is what makes running transcendental. It is what accounts for all of the "magical" properties of running. It is the loss of play that makes people depressed, lethargic, overly serious and set in their ways. To some, adult vices, such as abuse of alcohol, excessive TV-watching, and smoking, are substitutes for play. The ideal approach to running is as a child approaches play—with enthusiasm, a sense of promise, going to it each day and having it be fresh.

George Sheehan has described this, the ideal way to run: "Bringing to that running, that play, the attitude of a child, the perception of a poet. Being a beginner with a beginner's mind, a beginner's heart and a beginner's body."

It is this play aspect that acts so strongly on the personality of the runner; it is the joy of play, and its subtle effect on personality, that puts our psyche in order.

Play has a very important, though often neglected, psychological purpose.

". . . Play serves children and even adults," wrote Frank and Theresa Caplan in their book, *The Power of Play*. ". . . It can help to strengthen personality, encourage interpersonal relations, further creativity and the joy of living and advance learning."

The return of play sometimes very quickly erases adult problems and doubts. Debra J. was better able to play with her children after she started running than before.

Running is invigorating play, and as the Caplans write, "play is a happy activity which begins in delight and ends in wisdom." Running is the private play world, in which anything is possible, in which tangible boundaries are temporarily, joyously transcended.

Let yourself go out and play.

YOUR OWN PROGRAM

This book is about gaining a deeper appreciation for what you do, namely running.

Running isn't just a temporary enjoyment. If approached in a personal, relaxed manner, as this book has discussed, running can be a way to contentment, to becoming younger mentally, to regenerating old goals and ideals.

Use whatever forms of relaxation, meditation, Zen, and spiritual ideas that work best with your running. That is your program. Your coach is your intuition.

Like many beginning runners who never realize that there is more to this activity than choosing the right shoes and stopwatch and running for thirty minutes each day, I initially approached running in a fashion that, because of its emphasis on goals and long-term satisfaction, led to quitting.

The aim here isn't to see how far you can run or how fast, or to find someone's ideal schedule to follow. It's to develop an approach that is personally fulfilling and will keep you going.

Joe Henderson, who calls himself a "lifer," cites the example of Vladimar Kuts, winner of two gold medals at the 1956 Olympics, who quit running when he quit competition, began smoking, gained a hundred pounds, and died of a heart attack at age forty-eight.

"I'm not saying that running is the road to immortality," Henderson wrote in *Jog, Run, Race*:

> Vladimar Kuts might have died of a heart attack at forty-eight even if he had kept running the extra twenty years. The sad thing in his, as in a lot of less publicized cases, was that he seemed so anxious to get rid of an activity which apparently had been geared to him. Something in the way he approached his running wouldn't let him go on once his success was past.

HABIT

The secret to the fountain of youth, to feeling and being what you want to be, and, probably, the secret to almost everything in our existence, is habit. This book is about habits, about how to approach life in a new way. We tend to approach most new things in an old manner. This is because we act out of habit.

All habits are changeable and removable. First, though, you have to know that they exist and that there is something wrong with them. Then you can replace them with better habits. At the core of inner-directed Total Running is the substitution of positive habits for old negative habits.

Said Little Rock, Arkansas, runner Roger B., "I got rid of a lot of bad habits through running and just naturally seemed to acquire a lot of good ones."

Many people have habits that are leading them to an early death. They are too tense, too sedentary, too result-oriented. Total Running can change these things and save their lives.

As the case of Debra J. revealed, a joyless life-style is unnecessary, but may be habitual. Debra didn't enjoy the way she lived for three years, but found it difficult to break out of her habits. Running acted as a sudden push.

Seventy-nine percent of the runners polled said they run in part to relieve tension. These are people who have seen the habit that tension can become and don't like it. They have found out how to break this habit—by running.

In *You're Younger Than You Think*, Lelord Kordel explained how the habits that are our life-style often become dangerous, even suicidal, without our being able to do anything about them.

> Rushing gets to be a habit. Tension becomes a way of life. . . . Tenseness is contagious. It isn't easy to stay calm in a tension-charged atmosphere. Tight muscles are always painful. The tense person is constantly on edge, strained, ready to go into action. Muscle tightness, accompanied by excessive alertness or apprehension, produces a headache. Tenseness becomes a habit and such a headache can be painfully persistent. . . . Tension is a warning sign of a health crack-up. Americans work too hard and expect too much of themselves and others. . . . Disregard your mounting tenseness until you become mentally and physically worn out and you invite a nervous breakdown. Nine million Americans a year do exactly that. Leading psychiatrists state that a man does not break down from overwork but from his attitude toward his work.

Total Running, by improving attitude and ameliorating habits, prevents tension from becoming overwhelming.

When you practice Total Running, you acknowledge your subconscious and bring yourself better in touch with it. More stringent thinkers often ignore their subconscious, their feelings and intuitions; they don't have a complete understanding of themselves.

All of this is changeable. Worry has been shown to be mostly habit, resulting from lack of self-understanding. A recent study at the University of Wisconsin determined that 40 percent of people's worries are over things that never happen, more than 30 percent are things that happened in the past and can't be changed, 22 percent of worries are over petty, unnecessary fears, and only 8 percent of what we worry about is serious.

We are like this because no matter how intelligent we might become, we are still going to act from habit, and our habits may have nothing to do with our true essence or our intelligence or what we want to be doing. Our habits may, in fact, be detrimental to all of these things. Only by altering our habits can we become what we believe we can be. It is lack of self-knowledge that prevents us from changing our habits. Our habits are what determine how soon and how fast we age. With the total approach to running comes a greater self-knowledge that can change our habits and slow the wear on our bodies and minds that causes premature aging.

EXPERIMENT

The summer before my senior year in high school I needed to develop a strong endurance background for the upcoming cross-country season. But rather than plod along the same neighborhood streets every day, another runner and I decided to run to the beach—160 miles away. We made it in four and a half days, camping by the side of the road, and stopping every few miles at gas stations for drinks of water.

This is just one example of what you can do with running. To keep running interesting, you should have the urge to experiment with it, to try unusual runs. In *The Runner's Handbook*, Jack Shepherd talks of taking a "crazy run" once a week and his co-author Bob Glover says he goes on a weekly "animal run," in which he runs with wild animal abandon.

Try as much as you can with running. Race traffic. Sprint up impossible hills. Run along the ocean's edge in three feet of water. Run backwards. Run barefoot. Carry a transistor radio. Run with friends and harmonize. Run to work. Run to the store. Experiment.

CREATIVE RHYTHM

The state of mind that is developed during inner-directed running is similar to that of the artist. One becomes less concerned with time and obligations and more concerned with one's perceptions, with feeling and understanding.

The rhythm of the average adult is often very mechanical. He thrives on a daily schedule; he plans his spare hours in advance or else spends them in procrastination. The adult is dominated by habits and routines. He can look ahead two weeks and know pretty much what he'll be doing on a given day, perhaps even what he'll be thinking. He plots out his future, then carries out that plan.

This programmed thinking retards the spontaneity you had when you were younger and, more essentially, often takes away the joy in your life. But as the case of Debra J. illustrated, this joy can be recaptured.

In a creative rhythm you aren't constantly thinking about your life in terms of a plan and a schedule; instead, you can be surprised and fascinated by your own imagination. You can feel simple and true emotion. This is what running seems to give back to those who say their lives have been changed through it. And it is the goal of Total Running to burrow to the creative, artistic quality in us.

When approached solely as exercise, running only reinforces mechanical, programmed thinking. Then you are concerned foremost with finishing, with running a specific distance or for a specific number of minutes. But when you are able to forsake the mechanics of running and *feel* what you are doing, rather than just achieving it and getting it over with, then the running experience can change your way of thinking. You will suddenly be aware of the smells of the earth, the feel of the breeze, the euphoria of freedom; feelings that have no place, really, in a programmed life-style based on achieving rather than experiencing. You may suddenly see beyond your barriers of skepticism and realize that joy can be found in something as basic as running through a park on an autumn afternoon.

Jonathan W., a runner from Hollywood, Florida, gave an explanation of how running reintegrates a person with his creative rhythms: "I don't know if it's the running itself that is so effective, or the things it does. It's the things

a runner sees and feels on the run. He could probably get
a similar result from taking a walk or riding horses or riding a bicycle. It's that mixing with the physical elements
and the good simple feelings it produces. It's the good
feeling you get when you're finished. You feel like you've
done something. Not accomplished anything, really, but
experienced something."

This pinpoints the difference between the two basic approaches you can take with running. With the more programmed approach you run and collect mileage. You can
record the mileage and come back to it several months,
or years, later, and you may be pleased with what you've
accumulated.

But this often detracts from the joy of the actual experience. When you can forget the context and just think of
where you are, something happens. You experience the
run itself, as you may never have before. And sometimes a
revolution begins in your thinking.

When you don't accept limits of time or distance, you can
run not for goals but for feelings; you can run for as long or
as short a time as you want, as fast or as slow. You can run
not because you have something to achieve or to prove,
but because it is a natural, pleasing activity. You can think
not of how the run will look recorded in your training log,
but how it feels while it is happening. You don't stare at
the sidewalk and make up games in your mind to pass the
time; you can look at the sky, the trees, the buildings, and
run for whatever amount of time feels right. You don't get
a feeling of relief when you finish a run, but a sense of
satisfaction from the experience. You don't make running
an obligation for which you must set aside time, but instead

you run when you want to and enjoy it while it is happening.

For many whose thinking changes through running, the transformation is joyful and permanent. It goes against the grain of the mechanical rhythm most of us are used to, but it allows us to see that a lot is missed through mechanical rhythm. This is an artistic rhythm, in which feeling becomes more important and order less. That is the basic reason some people say running has made them younger again: it has torn them from their rhythm of order, blended them with reality, let them feel moments rather than just pass through them.

Dr. George Sheehan wrote about this in *Running and Being*:

> The artist, especially the poet, has always known . . . that time shortens and lengthens without regard to the minute hand. Knows that we have a beat foreign to this Greenwich metronome. Knows also there is an ebb and flow to the day that escapes the clock, but not us. And realizes that this rhythm, this tempo, is something peculiar to each individual, as personal and unchallenging as his fingerprints.

The artist knows this. The scientist has proved it. In *Biological Rhythms of Psychiatry and Medicine*, Bertram S. Brown writes:

> Rhythm is as much a part of our structure as our flesh and bones. Most of us are dimly aware that we fluctuate in energy, mood, well-being and performance each day, and that there are longer, more subtle variations each week, each month, each season, each year." . . . Life, except for a favored few, like poets and children and athletes and saints, is pretty much

of a bore. Given the choice, most of us would give up the reality of today for the memory of yesterday or the fantasy of tomorrow. We desire to live anywhere but in the present.

Running makes people young by putting them back in the present.

BIBLIOGRAPHY

Andrews, Valerie. *The Psychic Power of Running.* New York: Rawson Associates, 1978.

Batten, Jack. *The Complete Jogger.* New York: Harcourt Brace Jovanovich, 1977.

Blofeld, John, tr. *The Zen Teaching of Huang Po: On the Transmission of the Mind.* New York: Grove Press, 1959.

Bristol, Claude. *The Magic of Believing.* New York: Prentice-Hall, 1948.

Brown, Bertram S. *Biological Rhythms of Psychiatry and Medicine.*

Caplan, Frank, and Theresa Caplan. *The Power of Play.* New York: Anchor Press, 1973.

Collingwood, T. R. "The Effects of Physical Training Upon Behavior and Self-Attitudes." *Journal of Clinical Psychology,* 1972.

Cooper, Kenneth. *Aerobics.* New York: Bantam, 1968.

Cornillier, Pierre-Émile. *The Survival of the Soul and Its Evolution After Death.* New York: Krishna Press.

Cox, Harvey. *Feast of Fools.* Cambridge, Mass.: Harvard University Press, 1969.

Crookall, Robert. *The Techniques of Astral Projection.* London: Aquarian Press, 1970.

Doyle, Arthur Conan. *The Edge of the Unknown.* New York: G. P. Putnam's, 1930.

Eischens, Roger and John Greist. *Run to Reality.* Thornwood, N.Y.: Caroline House, 1978.

Fixx, James F. *The Complete Book of Running.* New York: Random House, 1977.

Folkins, Carlyle H. "Effects of Physical Training on Mood." *Journal of Clinical Psychology,* April 1976.

Glasser, William. *Positive Addiction.* New York: Harper and Row, 1976.

Glover, Bob and Jack Shepherd. *The Runner's Handbook.* New York: Penguin, 1978.

Goldstein, Joseph. *The Experience of Insight: A Natural Unfolding.* Santa Cruz, Calif.: Unity Press, 1976.

Greenhouse, Herbert. *The Astral Journey.* Garden City, N.Y.: Doubleday, 1975.

Hardy, Alister, Robert Harvie, and Arthur Koestler. *The Challenge of Chance: A Mass Experiment in Telepathy and Its Outcome.* New York: Random House, 1974.

Henderson, Joe. *Jog, Run, Race.* Mountain View, Calif.: World Publications, 1977.

BIBLIOGRAPHY

————. *The Long-Run Solution.* Mountain View, Calif.: World Publications, 1976.

Henning, Joel. *Holistic Running: Beyond the Threshold of Fitness.* New York: Atheneum, 1978.

Hewitt, James. *Yoga.* London: Hodder and Stoughton Ltd., 1960.

Higdon, Hal. "Can Running Cure Mental Illness?" *Runner's World,* January 1978.

————. "Is Running a Religious Experience?" *Runner's World,* May 1978.

Humphreys, Christmas. *Concentration and Meditation.* Baltimore: Penguin, 1970.

Jackson, Ian. *Yoga and the Athlete.* Mountain View, Calif.: World Publications, 1975.

Jencks, Beata. *Your Body: Biofeedback at Its Best.* Chicago: Nelson-Hall, 1977.

Karlgaard, Richard. *The Last Word on Running.* Thornwood, N.Y.: Caroline House, 1978.

Kordell, Lelord. *You're Younger Than You Think.* New York: Putnam, 1976.

Kostrubala, Thaddeus. *The Joy of Running.* Philadelphia and New York: J. P. Lippincott Company, 1976.

Kubose, Gyomay M. *Zen Koans.* Chicago: Henry Regnery Co., 1973.

Lilliefors, Jim. *The Running Mind.* Mountain View, Calif.: World Publications, 1978.

Merton, Thomas. *Mystics and Zen Masters.* New York: Delta Books, 1967.

Monroe, Robert. *Journeys Out of the Body.* Garden City, N.Y.: Doubleday, 1971.

Muhl, Anita M. *Automatic Writing: An Approach to the Subconscious.* New York: Helix Press, 1963.

Muldoon, S. and H. Carrington. *The Phenomena of Astral Projection.* London: Rider, 1929.

Nelson, Geoffrey. *Spiritualism and Society.* New York: Schocken Books, 1969.

Nhat Hanh, Thich. *Zen Keys.* Garden City, N.Y.: Doubleday, Anchor Press, 1974.

Nideffer, Robert M. *The Inner Athlete: Mind Plus Muscle for Winning.* New York: Thomas Y. Crowell, 1976.

Niebuhr, Reinhold. *Does Civilization Need Religion?* New York: Macmilllan, 1927.

Reymond, Lizelle. *To Live Within.* Garden City, N.Y.: Doubleday, 1971.

Rhine, Joseph Banks. *New World of the Mind.* New York: William Sloane Associates, 1953.

Rolf, Ida. *What in the World Is Rolfing?* Santa Monica, Calif.: Dennis-Landman, 1975.

Roberts, Jane. *The Nature of Personal Reality.* Englewood Cliffs, N.J.: Prentice-Hall, Inc., 1974.

Rohe, Fred. *The Zen of Running.* New York and Berkeley: Random House-Bookworks, 1974.

Rogo, D. Scott (ed.). *Mind Beyond the Body: The Mystery of ESP Projection.* New York: Penguin Books, 1978.

Rose, Steven. *Human Consciousness.* New York: Random House, 1971.

Ross, Nancy Wilson, ed. *The World of Zen.* New York: Vintage, 1960.

Runner's World, Editors of. *The Complete Runner.* Mountain View, Calif.: World Publications, 1974.

———. *New Guide to Distance Running.* Mountain View, Calif.: World Publications, 1978.

Schloegl, Irmgard. *The Wisdom of Zen Masters.* New York: New Directions, 1976.

Selye, Hans. *The Stress of Life.* New York: McGraw-Hill, 1956.

Sheehan, George. *Doctor Sheehan on Running.* Mountain View, Calif.: World Publications, 1975.

———. *Running and Being.* New York: Simon and Schuster, 1978.

Shestak, Robert. *Handbook of Physical Therapy.* New York: Springer Publishing, 1956.

Spino, Michael. *Beyond Jogging.* Millbrae, Calif.: Celestial Arts, 1976.

———. *Running Home.* Milbrae, Calif.: Celestial Arts, 1977.

Taylor, John. *The Superminds: A Scientist Looks at the Paranormal.* New York: Viking Press, 1975.

Thien-An, Thich. *Zen Philosophy, Zen Practice.* Buddhi, ed. Emeryville, Calif.: Dharma Publishing, 1975.

Toffler, Alvin. *Future Shock.* New York: Random House, 1970.

Vonnegut, Kurt. *Slaughterhouse-Five.* New York: Delacorte Press, 1969.

White, Stewart Edward. *The Unobstructed Universe.* New York: E. P. Dutton, 1940.